The Green Book

Writings on Irish Gothic,
Supernatural and Fantastic Literature

Issue 2
Samhain 2013

Edited by

Brian J. Showers

The Swan River Press
Dublin, Ireland
MMXIII

The Green Book
Issue 2, Samhain 2013
edited by Brian J. Showers

Published by
The Swan River Press
Dublin, Ireland
in October, MMXIII

www.swanriverpress.ie
brian@swanriverpress.ie

Set in Garamond by Ken Mackenzie

ISSN 2009-6089

The Green Book 2
is limited to 350 copies.

Contents

Editor's Note

As I write this, the newly constructed bridge spanning the River Liffey here in Dublin remains yet unnamed. The short-list is comprised of five Dubliners and includes trade union-ist Rosie Hackett, who participated in the 1913 Lockout; and camogie player Kay Mills. But one name among them will stand out to devotees of horror and gothic literature the world over: Bram Stoker.

Since *Dracula* was chosen for One City, One Book in 2009, public awareness of Stoker's connections with Ireland (he was born in Dublin, so he was!), and Irish acceptance of his importance to world literature, has approached fever pitch. In addition to being short-listed for the new bridge, Dublin now hosts an annual Bram Stoker Festival, the first of which was held in 2012 to mark the centenary of Stoker's death; the illuminating "Lost Dublin Journal", edited by Elizabeth Miller and Dacre Stoker, saw publication; and Dublin UNESCO City of Literature proudly lists Stoker alongside Yeats, Shaw, Joyce, and Beckett. So too did the Stoker family rally to establish the Bram Stoker Estate, and embarked upon their mission to spread awareness of Bram Stoker's life and achievements—and with a man like Stoker, even leaving *Dracula* aside, there's much to explore.

But this interest in Stoker didn't happen overnight: efforts to "repatriate" the author of *Dracula* as a Dubliner started as early as 1980 with the founding of the Bram Stoker Society. The tireless efforts of its members perhaps culminated with the installation of a memorial plaque dedicated to Stoker on Kildare Street. I should also point out that the Society's journal, and its editorial decision to embrace the broader Irish fantastic, was a key influence on *The Green Book*'s similarly inclusive scope.

With Ireland's pivotal genre writer increasingly recognised in the Irish literary world, now is the perfect opportunity to champion and bring to the fore Ireland's other masters of the fantastic—their stories and novels.

The lead piece in this issue is Richard Dalby's fascinating overview of the work of satirist Mervyn Wall, whose novel *The Unfortunate Fursey* is a wrongly neglected classic that is invariably held in high-regard by those who have read it. Albert Power gives us the second instalment of his ongoing survey of Irish gothic literature, while Steve Gronert Ellerhof revisits Ray Bradbury's often overlooked Irish novel *Green Shadows, White Whale*. And finally, in addition to numerous book reviews, I am pleased to present Nicola Gordon Bowe's fascinating article on Lord Dunsany and his connections with the Irish Arts and Crafts Movement.

With Bram Stoker currently in the spotlight, now is the time to illuminate another gothic writer whose bicentenary we will celebrate next year. At the moment nothing official is planned by any local institution, so we may have to do it ourselves. Haven't guessed? How about a clue . . .

Brian J. Showers
Rathmines, Dublin
28 August 2013

Mervyn Wall:
Irish Author and Satirist

Richard Dalby

Mervyn Wall, who died on the 19th of May 1997, was an outstanding satirist and a master of comic fantasy whose work has often been favourably compared with that of Kenneth Grahame and J.R.R. Tolkien. His two richly textured masterpieces, *The Unfortunate Fursey* and its sequel, *The Return of Fursey,* published over half a century ago, established the lovable but ineffectual Brother Fursey as one of the great anti-heroes of fiction. Generations of readers have followed his journeys through the uproarious world of medieval Ireland, with its bizarre population of rapacious demons and vampires, witches and familiars, bishops and monks. Fursey is forever caught between the Devil and the equally devious rogues among his fellow clerics, and his adventures are all thinly veiled satires on modern Irish life.

Scribners's monumental study of *Supernatural Fiction Writers* (1985) includes chapters on nine Irish authors: Charles Maturin, Sheridan Le Fanu, Fitz-James O'Brien, Bram Stoker, Oscar Wilde, Lord Dunsany, James Stephens, Elizabeth Bowen—and Mervyn Wall. Wall's inclusion is quite fitting. Fursey and his incredible supporting cast of fantastic and supernatural characters deserve to be remembered alongside Melmoth, Dracula, Dorian Gray, and all the other memorable creations of Irish literature.

Mervyn Wall was born in Palmerston Road, Dublin, on 23rd August 1908, the son of a successful barrister. Like

James Joyce, he was educated at the Jesuit school, Belvedere College, and University College, Dublin, from which he received an arts degree in 1928. Whilst there, he served as head of the University's Dramatic Society and became a devotee of the Abbey Theatre. Between 1922 and 1924, he lived in Bonn, where he studied music and painting.

In the depression years of the early Thirties, there were very few good jobs available for B.A. graduates, and initially Wall worked as a clerk in the Agricultural Credit Corporation from 1930 to 1932. In 1934, he entered the Irish Civil Service where he spent fourteen dreary and monotonous years. This long period of stultifying routine, and of constant contact with boorish and uneducated officials, left an indelible mark upon Wall and his writing. He became all too familiar with the inconsistencies which riddled Irish government, and especially with the defensive role played there by the Knights of Columbanus—a secret society of Catholic laymen (including Wall's father) similar to the Freemasons and the Rotary Club.

Wall's first—and best-known—play, *Alarm Among the Clerks,* was probably the earliest Irish drama to show the terrible monotony and quiet despair that fill the life of the modern urban office worker. It premiered at the Peacock Theatre in April 1937, and was first published by the Richview Press in Dublin three years later. His second play, *The Lady in the Twilight* (set in West Wicklow), was first produced at the Abbey Theatre in May 1941, but did not achieve book publication until 1971.

Wall's first widely read work was a short story, "They Also Serve", which appeared in the July 1940 issue of *Harper's Magazine*. He wrote several other short stories for *Colliers, Argosy, Irish Writing,* and the *Capuchin Annual*, encompassing not only wry glimpses of Civil Service life, but also comic fantasies of the supernatural, including "Leo the Terror",

"The Demon Angler", "The Men Who Could Outstare Cobras", and "Metamorphosis of a Licensed Vintner" (aka "Hair on a Billiard Ball"). The "alcoholic" ghost story, "Cloonaturk" *(Argosy*; December 1947), was later reprinted in *Weird Tales* (Summer 1989). These short stories were eventually collected as *A Flutter of Wings* in 1974.

Mervyn Wall began working on his comic masterpiece, *The Unfortunate Fursey*, while recovering from an attack of pleurisy in 1945. The theme was originally inspired by an ancient library book (lacking the title-page) which he unearthed in Dublin—a translation of a French work on ghosts, demons, and witches, published around 1600. He was fascinated by the elaborate and ponderous language in which it set out the absurd medieval beliefs and superstitions connected with witchcraft, and also by all the monstrous but risible demons which hopped in and out of every page. This comic-strip medieval world provided Wall with the perfect opportunity to satirise the political and religious life of post-war Ireland.

Wall's book is set in the tenth century. His endearing anti-hero, the gentle but totally ineffectual and accident-prone Brother Fursey, is a lay brother at the monastery of Clonmacnoise. As the most inept member of the community, his main task is preparing edible roots in the kitchen, but he can't even carry out this simple task without cutting himself. In the first chapter, the Devil and all his minions assail the monastery for fifteen days. Haunted by "imps and ghouls, night fiends, goblins and all sorts of hellish phantoms", the holy monks managed to repulse these evil forces completely, whereupon the Devil decides to concentrate wholly on the weaker inhabitant: Fursey. As the assorted serpents, incubi and undraped females invade his cell, Fursey is petrified with fear and cannot pronounce the correct form of adjuration.

He is not only cast out into the world by the abbot, but also reluctantly married to an ancient crone (called The Old

Grey Mare) who is really a witch engaged in a battle to the death with the local wizard and church sexton. When she is defeated and fatally wounded, she tricks Fursey into a first (and final) kiss, and breathes her powers into him. The Old Grey Mare's most unwelcome gift is her familiar, Albert, a shaggy dog-like beast with bear paws who requires to be fed blood from a supernumerary nipple Fursey has acquired on his anatomy. As a completely untutored wizard, Fursey knows only how to ride a broomstick and to produce food and drink by tossing a rope over a beam or tree branch.

Fursey is always encountering demons like the irascible green monster known as Joe the Poltergeist, but a much greater threat is posed by the civil and religious authorities, both of which want to torture him and burn him at the stake. The trial scenes are highly satirical, containing such memorable lines as: "If the accused should be found not guilty after the evidence has been considered . . . we will start again at the beginning and accept his plea of guilty."

There is a rare idyllic interlude when Fursey falls in love with Maeve, the girl on whose father's farm he is working. After many fruitless attempts at accommodation with church and state, Fursey finally becomes fed up with Ireland. He ignites the thatch on the bishop's palace, swoops down on his broomstick to rescue Maeve just as she is about to marry someone else, and flies eastwards over "the crooked roads and the sluggishly rolling mountains of Ireland, the first of many exiles for whom a decent way of living was not to be had in their own country". There are similar scathing lines on nearly every page, although the author loved his country too much (if not its churchmen, bureaucrats, and politicians) ever to contemplate living in England or any other part of the world.

The Unfortunate Fursey was first published by the London-based Pilot Press in 1946, and was issued in the United States by Crown in 1947. It was reissued as a Helicon paperback (Dublin) in 1965. Although Wall sold the film rights to the novel, it has yet to be adapted for the screen. However, a musical version was staged at the Dublin Theatre Festival in 1964.

Its sequel, *The Return of Fursey* (Pilot Press, 1948), is every bit as good as—if not better—than the original. The story relates how Fursey loses Maeve and returns to Ireland to recover her from her erstwhile fiancée, Magnus; how he sells his soul to his old acquaintance the Devil; and how he eventually loses everything except his soul and his stoicism. Once again we encounter such characters as the unhelpful familiar, Albert, and the sorcerer Cuthbert, with many new characters like the wealthy Festus Wisenuts, George the Vampire, and a roistering crew of Vikings led by Sigurd the Skull Splitter. Comparing the Fursey stories with the best of Charlie Chaplin, Chekhov, or Sean O'Casey, Wall's biographer, Robert Hogan, has rightly observed that "the laughter is very akin to tears, and that quality is very akin to high art".

Unlike the first book, *The Return of Fursey* is richly enhanced by several missal-style illustrations by John Parsons which perfectly capture the flavour and robust humour of the magical Dark Ages. These illustrations are retained in the very welcome omnibus edition, *The Complete Fursey*, issued (in both hard- and paperback) by the Wolfhound Press in 1985.

Soon after *The Unfortunate Fursey* was published, Wall was transferred by the Civil Service from Dublin to Sligo, far away from all his literary and theatrical friends, and then onto an even more obscure post in Manorhamilton. Eventually, in 1948, after enduring fourteen long years in the Irish Civil Service, he joined the state radio station in Dublin, Radio Éireann, as a programme assistant in the general features department. In this congenial atmosphere, he not only regularly met Ireland's prominent literary personalities, but also the musician, Fanny Feehan, who became his wife in 1950. They had a son and three daughters.

He supplemented his small income by writing talks, documentaries, and book reviews, and by freelance broadcasting. Wall's radio series, Along Many a Mile, comprised seventy-two chatty, historical talks about the Irish countryside. Radio Éireann also produced his play, Wicklow Granite.

His feelings about the stultifying provincial surroundings he had recently endured in Sligo and Manorhamilton were duly reflected in his third novel, *Leaves for the Burning*, published by Methuen in 1952. The middle-aged hero of this book, Lucian Brewse Burke, is a low-grade County Council employee, and the plot centres around the attempts of four drunken friends to make the pilgrimage to Sligo, where W.B. Yeats's remains are to be re-interred in Drumcliffe Churchyard. Needless to say, they all fail to reach their destination.

The narrative, both hilarious and disturbing, was intended by Wall to give an exact picture of Ireland as it really was in 1952. The extent to which he fulfilled his ambition can be gauged from the review in *The Times Literary Supplement* (25 January 1952), which described the book as "a brilliantly amusing, bitter and occasionally sentimental novel about contemporary Ireland", adding that "it is notable for the way in which moral corruption blends indistinguishably into the atmosphere of Irish country life. Through the whole grotesque, comic parade of chicanery and superstition—the patriotic songs sung by crooks and parasites in public houses, the strike of road workers who refuse to cut down a fairy tree, the suicide who keeps his head inside the oven for half an hour without turning on the gas—Mr. Wall discovers a state of mind which is at once fantastic and curiously convincing."

The author's views on the country can be summed up by the adjectives he used in the first paragraph—"dull, dark, aching, disagreeable, horrid, dreadful . . . " John Broderick (author of several powerful novels about Irish provincial life) described *Leaves for the Burning* as "the best Irish novel ever written", and it won a Danish competition for the outstanding European novel of 1952. The American edition was published by Devin Adair (1952), and the work was reissued twenty years later by the Irish University Press.

Wall's next novel, *No Trophies Raise* (Methuen, 1956), was even more bitingly satirical about political bureaucracy. The lead character, "Pig Feed" Sam Welply, is a brilliant embodiment of venality and base cunning. (He is the forebear of many similar characters in modern Irish stories and TV programmes like the BBC's *Ballykissangel*.) Branching out from his successful pig-feed business into the booming tourist trade, Welply builds a luxury hotel by the Lake of Killarney. When he suggests to the government that the hotel should be opened by an international celebrity, the Minister for Arts and Crafts proposes Albert Thomas Hand, "probably the greatest philosopher the world has produced in the last hundred years". In fact, Hand is really a poverty-stricken minor civil servant in the Minister's own department. He dies of pneumonia soon after delivering his speech and is secretly buried in a pauper's grave to avoid public embarrassment.

A lengthy sub-plot involves Sam's neophyte son, Eugene Welply, who is honest enough to deplore his father's immoral tactics, but is finally too weak to resist the attractions of money and security. This sub-plot allowed Wall free reign to introduce several satirical topics, including the aforementioned Knights of Columbanus, which did little to endear Wall to the brotherhood!

Curiously, most obituaries stated that Mervyn Wall's own middle names were "Eugene Welply", but this is not confirmed by earlier sources, or by Robert Hogan's biography. It may be conjectured that Eugene and Sam Welply were loosely based on Mervyn Wall and his own father, whose membership of the Knights of Columbanus was instrumental in securing his son's appointment to the Civil Service in the early 1930s.

Several London critics declared that the satire in *No Trophies Raise* was greatly exaggerated and overdone. However, an anonymous reviewer in *The Dublin Magazine* nobly defended Wall from this charge, remarking that "those English critics who have protested that the fantasy is too extravagant might profitably examine the correspondence columns of Irish newspapers, and the reports of borough and town council meetings".

Overall, Wall's reputation as an important writer and satirist was enhanced, rather than harmed, by the heated debates prompted by *No Trophies Raise,* and in the following year (1957), the distinguished writer, Seán Ó Faoláin, secured his appointment as chief executive of the Irish Arts Council. Wall also remained busy writing articles and reviews for Dublin periodicals such as *Hibernia, Irish Writing, The Irish Times*, and *The Bell*, and was for many years radio critic of the *Dublin Evening Press.*

Wall liked to bathe each day at Sandycove, by the Martello tower which had been made famous by James Joyce's *Ulysses*, and he wrote a short, whimsical history of the spot entitled *Forty Foot Gentlemen Only* (Allen Figgis, 1962). This was illustrated by Frank Foley.

One of his fellow swimmers at Sandycove was Dr. John Redmond, chairman of the Revenue Commissioners. In 1969, the Irish finance minister, Charles Haughey, announced a scheme to exempt from income tax all creative artists whose work was of "cultural merit". Redmond was appointed to select the worthy beneficiaries, and after a swim at Sandycove one day he enlisted Wall's help in the project. Wall speedily obliged with a list of 150 artists and sculptors, and twenty-seven writers, including all his fellow members of the Irish Academy of Letters. Every one of his nominations was accepted by Redmond.

The Arts Council was then made sole arbiter of this scheme, which meant that all future applicants had to pass the scrutiny of Mervyn Wall, in his role as chief executive. He was assisted by his wife Fanny, who suggested several eligible musicians and composers.

Wall was also able to accommodate British writers like Frederick Forsyth and Len Deighton, who had acquired homes in Ireland following the introduction of punitive tax rates by the Labour Government. By 1972, there were 338 artists and authors in the scheme. During his simultaneous tenure as Secretary of the Irish Academy of Letters, Wall was able to secure a regular income for this organisation, and arranged for the award of an annual prize of £250 for promising young writers.

In 1974, Wall retired as Secretary of both the Arts Council and the Academy of Letters, continuing to work as a busy journalist and reviewer. In that same year, Talbot Press published the best of his short stories in a collection entitled *A Flutter of Wings*.

Over the next four years, he concentrated on his last major literary work, *Hermitage*. This was Mervyn Wall's longest novel, a superbly realistic portrait of Ireland, as presented by the tragic murderer, Tony Langton, in his prison journal—"the final hermitage of a defeated man". (Wall himself once declared that his pipe-dream was "a long term in a quiet prison to enable full attention to be given to literary pursuits".)

The book covered fifty years of Langton's—and Irish—life, and again sharply satirised the vagaries of the Civil Service. It portrayed a world in conflict, and the hero's social descent is both a lament for, and an indictment of, the class and morality which he has inherited.

Wall intended that *Hermitage* would be his *magnum opus*, and took great care honing the text during the late 1970s. In this, he received much prodding and bullying from his wife, who dispatched him to remote parts of the Irish countryside, well away from the distractions of Dublin, until he phoned home to announce the completion of a chapter. In this way, the long, rambling narrative became a wonderfully tight and compelling novel of 120,000 words.

It was originally serialised in the *Journal of Irish Literature* in 1978-79, before being issued in both hard- and paperback by Wolfhound Press in 1982. The cover features a photograph of Langton sitting at his writing desk on a desolate stone jetty looking out to sea.

Wall's celebrated sense of fun and fantasy (almost entirely absent from *Hermitage* and *Leaves for the Burning*) returned with great effect in *The Garden of Echoes*, which also made its debut in the *Journal of Irish Literature*. (Together with a speech, an interview and a reprinting of *Alarm Among the Clerks*, it made up the "Mervyn Wall Double Number", dated January-May 1982.) The journal was edited by Robert Hogan, the author's biographer and main champion in America.

Subtitled, "A Fable for Children and Grown-Ups", *The Garden of Echoes* was a Christmas tale about the attempted assassination of Santa Claus, and was described by the author as "a sort of up-to-date *Alice in Wonderland*" or "Narnia" chronicle. Wall had actually written this story in 1958 for his two young daughters, Drusilla and Aileen, to whom the book is dedicated, and who also feature as the story's two heroines.

Early in the narrative, Ann and Beatrice find a strange new world behind their father's bookcase. Crawling further into the opening between the books, "they came to the entrance of a long passage and found that they could stand up without any danger of hitting their heads against the shelf above. The passage seemed to be very long and ran between two rows of books much taller than the girls themselves. Every now and then there was a book which had gilt-edged pages, and these books reflected a queer golden light which lit the passage in the same way as street lamps light a street at night."

Reaching the end of the passage, the girls suddenly find themselves in the open air. After encountering a toy shop owned by a money-grabbing pig, they proceed on their journey across "The Fields We Know", through "The Magic Wood" to "Snake and Ladder Mountain", and beyond "Far Away" to "The Country of Frost and Snow". Apart from the pig, they encounter many other colourful characters, such as the schoolteacher, Mr. Baboon, the eccentric Crooked Man and his crooked cat, and the King of the Giants.

Their adventures symbolise the difficulties which the girls will someday have to face in the adult world. As Wall noted in his short preface: "When I had finished writing these adventures of two small sisters, one seven and the other five years old, and sat back to consider what I had done, I decided that it was a satire on adults from the child's point of view, and in the concluding pages, the author's satire on children because they would themselves be adults one day. On thinking about it in later days, I realised that it was more—it was in fact the writer's protest against the inevitable passing of childhood."

The first Irish edition of this ingenious fable, which is surely destined to become a classic of children's literature, was published by Fingal Books in 1988—coinciding with the author's eightieth birthday. There were simultaneous hard- and paperback editions.

Wall found too many distractions in Dublin and at his home in Castlepark Road, Sandycove, to concentrate on any more major literary endeavours. Nevertheless, he continued to work on new stories, including "The Odious Generation", which includes a description of a drug-induced hallucination.

He also remained busy with lectures and reviews, and in

November 1989 he gave an illuminating talk on his literary career (with special emphasis on Fursey) to the Bram Stoker Society in Dublin. The text of this lecture was reprinted in two issues of the Society journal, edited by the current writer.

Mervyn Wall died on 19th May 1997 (a year after his wife) in his beloved Dublin, where he had resided and worked—with only two short breaks—for the whole of his life.

Wall may not be the weightiest of Ireland's many great writers, but he is certainly a distinctive one. His wonderfully satirical novels are sure to last, and in Brother Fursey he created an unforgettable comic character to rank alongside those of Swift, Wilde, and Flann O'Brien. If Ireland is undoubtedly the "land of saints and sinners", then Fursey reveals that there's a whole lot more to the country besides. In the words of the abbot of Clonmacnoise: "In Ireland, anything may happen to anyone anywhere and at any time, and it usually does."

Towards an Irish Gothic
Part Two

Albert Power

Chapter IV: Gothic Grapplings in the Longer Form

". . . never did I know a man that did not delight in fostering the worst brier that he had planted; never do I remember a man who could forgive the innocent he had injured."

– Cullen

The publication, in the summer of 1794, of Ann Radcliffe's four-volume mystery romance *The Mysteries of Udolpho* was to be a culminating point in the heretofore snail-paced development of the gothic novel. It is the first specimen that could justly aspire to the status of literature. And it was, to boot, inordinately long. To the devices of medieval gothicism embodied by Walpole and Leland, Ann Radcliffe shackled the structure and interior style of the novel of romantic sensibility. In this she can be said to hark to somewhat of the manner of Samuel Richardson, against whose labyrinthine mastodons in epistolary prose the early and terser gothic novels were somewhat in the nature of a palace revolt. The delicately-spun sub-theme of purity in the uncorrupted primitive exhales no meagre whiff of the wisdom of Rousseau, and in her tale's tragic intensity Radcliffe evinces respectful fealty to Shakespeare's dramas, its darker points alluringly touched with an alert, grue-laden particularity reminiscent of Milton. All mediated through a carefully-woven tapestry of the sublime in nature and architecture, that demonstrates to resplendent purpose the merit of Edmund Burke's *Philosophical Enquiry* as an aid to enduring effect in the longer-form fictions of dark romance.

The essence of the plot of *The Mysteries of Udolpho*—which for the first time in gothic writing involves much narrative complexity—is a shadowed enlargement of the basic story device in *The Adventures of Miss Sophia Berkley*. Emily St. Aubert is a young lady of demure virtue and exquisite sensibility, who lives with her parents in the countryside of Gascony during the late 1500s. Her mother dying early in the book, Emily embarks on a restorative tour with her father, on which she meets Valancourt, who soon becomes her admirer. Preliminary vestiges of mystery appear in amorous signs from an unknown enthusiast found in a fishing lodge that Emily frequents, and by evidence of her father's secret emotion over a miniature of a woman who is not his wife. After Valancourt proceeds on his travels, Emily's father dies. She becomes the ward of a mercenary aunt, who marries the dour, covetous Montoni. His remote and sinister Apennine fortress is the Udolpho of the title. The extensive outworking of the story concerns Emily's eventual reunion with a somewhat life-sullied Valancourt, the arrival and dispatch of an alternative admirer, and discovery of the link between a former inhabitant of Udolpho and a buried tragic history in Emily's own family. There are many divergences along the way, and not a few glintings from the supernatural, all which turn out to have human—even if very unlikely human—agency.

Where Ann Radcliffe is perhaps unique, and most certainly distinctive, in her contribution to the gothic, is her painstaking (and, be it confessed, sometimes painful) and frequent elaborations of an atmosphere of the awesome based on both visual and physical encounters in nature. This is more than mere scene-painting, and in terms of density of application, regularity of recurrence and evocativeness of her prose, enables the author construct a vast-arced panoply of the profound extending through the book that touches at times upon the numinous. There *are* limitations, of course. This may be literature, but hardly literature in its most exalted state. Plot meanderings are profuse, and occasionally the tactics resorted to to evoke terror of the otherworldly are spurious beyond acceptance. Too often is the reader lured down a tenebrous back-alley of story that features vivid depictions of lonely scenes and awe-stirring encounters, which lead nowhere. There are cumbrous moments of severance of the narrative point of view: so that, in one case, Emily sees a letter, whose contents are crucial to the story but not revealed to the reader for hundreds of pages; then there is an alcove vision behind a curtain, that quickly causes our heroine to faint, which very much later is disclosed as one thing, and at the end as quite something else. But to judge in terms of overall effect—Ann Radcliffe's is an achievement of higher order than any heretofore.

To this epoch of the gothic novel also, Irish letters made no mean contribution. The principal protagonist was Waterford-born Regina Maria Roche. Coeval with Ann Radcliffe, though living far longer, this lady's heyday of contribution to the novel of gothic romance was, similarly, the 1790s, and is exemplified by her two most enduring works: *The Children of the Abbey* (1796) and *Clermont* (1798).

The Children of the Abbey adopts a storyline conceit similar to *The Mysteries of Udolpho*, though, interestingly, Regina Roche's book is set, not on the continent of Europe, but in multiple locations throughout Wales, Ireland, and Scotland, with some of the action taking place in London. Amanda Fitzalan is our beautiful young heroine of matchless virtue, exquisite sensibility, and infinite patience. She is cast very much in the mould of her mother, Lady Malvina Dunreath of Dunreath Abbey in Scotland (the abbey of the title), who married in secret the impecunious but worthily descended Fitzalan, whose family is Irish. The story opens after the death of Amanda's mother, when her father has had to dispatch her to a former governess in Wales to evade the lascivious clutches of Colonel Belgrave. In the meantime, Fitzalan has taken up a post as agent to the Co. Antrim demesne of the wealthy, or supposedly so, Lord Cherbury. While in Wales, Amanda meets and become enamoured of handsome, courteous, and courtly Lord Mortimer. Their passion is reciprocal and advances to a state of mutual disclosure before Amanda discovers that Mortimer is the son of Lord Cherbury. This introduces the first of nigh innumerable complications which, one after one, block the longed for union of the two lovers. Like *Udolpho*, the novel abounds in subplots, one of which concerns the plight of Amanda's brother, Oscar, the admired of whose heart has been sneakily enticed to wed—yes, the selfsame nefarious Colonel Belgrave who lusted for his sister. Spanning the entire story is the tragedy of the disenfranchisement of Amanda and Oscar from their Dunreath inheritance through the contrivance of the second wife of the earl, the children's grandfather. Hence are they the "children of the abbey", though little enough time in this over-long rodomontade is spent there.

Like Ann Radcliffe, Regina Roche displays a masterful competence of control over her hugely deployed material; and although there are elements of the story that seem to wend nowhere (as in *Udolpho*), nowhere is found inconsistency, though much would fight a hard case to be felt probable. Unlike the better-known writer, however, Regina Roche peoples her novel with too vast a cast, too intricate a welter of plotlines, the cumulative effect of which is to pile obstacle after obstacle against the nuptials of Amanda and Mortimer, to so bewildering and unlikely a degree that there must be occasions—maybe many—when the reader is driven to wonder at the point of it all.

Herein lies the principal difference between the *oeuvre* of Ann Radcliffe and that of Regina Roche. For all of its entangled elaborations, *Udolpho* is firmly a gothic romance, though pitched somewhat in the style and vaunting the typical concerns of a novel of sensibility. By contrast, *The Children of the Abbey* is, from first to last, a novel of sensibility with rare elements of the gothic. From the perspective of a survey of the gothic in Ireland, this limits the exaltedness of that place which might otherwise be claimed by Regina Maria Roche. Too often, scenes of the grim and grand in nature or the gloomy in architecture are slickly fitted in with a view to atmosphere. There is nothing of course wrong with this, but the atmosphere so created is background rather than pervasive as succeeded in being achieved by Ann Radcliffe. Too often also—in *Children* and in *Clermont*—are references to sights described as *both* profound and beautiful, which shows a blurring of the bounds of the Edmund Burke aesthetic or else a falsification of the precept that lies at the core of the case urged by his *Philosophical Enquiry*.

Much of Regina Roche's gothic-type scene-painting in *Children of the Abbey* displays a loose-limbed flakiness that betrays provenance of short-term intended effect. Witness this darkness-to-light picture of a ruined island church in Fermanagh's Lough Erne, decided on as the site of an entertainment for some army officers:

" . . . the old trees in groups formed a thick canopy overhead, and the ivy that crept along the walls filled up many of the niches where the windows had formerly been . . . the long succession of arches which composed the body of the chapel were in many places covered with creeping moss, and scattered over with wall-flowers, blue hare-bells, and other spontaneous productions of nature, while between them were placed seats and breakfast-tables, ornamented in a fanciful manner."

In truth, *The Children of the Abbey* can boast only one scene of genuine gothic effectiveness—but this one is a masterpiece! It occurs, three-quarters' way through the book, when Amanda, at last arriving in Dunreath Abbey, in the guise of a paid tutor under an assumed name, comes face to face with the imprisoned Lady Dunreath in a cordoned-off upstairs wing, and takes her for a ghost. This scene is drawn by Roche with impressive dexterity, and leaves an effect so lasting that it is hard not to conceive that the image of an aging woman with a wicked secret, locked away in an upstairs room, must have spurred a like device in J.S. Le Fanu's early long story "Chapter in the History of a Tyrone Family", which reappeared in his later novel *The Wyvern Mystery* and may have been a prototype for elements in Charlotte Brontë's *Jane Eyre*.

It should not be supposed that on all points of comparison Regina Maria Roche appears to disadvantage by the side of Ann Radcliffe. From an Irish point of view, it is refreshing to find in a novel at least part-ways gothic scenes that are set and vividly described in the water-run loveliness of Co. Fermanagh, or which feature the austere, brooding coastline of that part of Co. Antrim that faces towards Scotland. Likewise, to be brought into hovels of the peasantry, where unlike with those of Ann Radcliffe, the fare on offer is a basin of boiled potatoes and a jug of buttermilk. The convent of St. Catharine near Amanda's father's Irish residence of Castle Carberry is rather more accurately evoked than kindred continental establishments in the fictions of Ann Radcliffe, and the jovially bumptious Catholic priest

Fr. O'Gallaghan (a man of perhaps unlikely, but doubtless genuine, jollification during the so-called penal laws) is fore-runner to a comparable cleric who joins in the often amusements of the Royal Irish Artillery in J.S. Le Fanu's splendid 1861 novel of old Chapelizod, set a hundred years earlier, *The House by the Churchyard*. Surely it is rather more than mere coincidence that Le Fanu should designate *his* rotund Roman churchman Fr. Roach!

Perhaps most important of all standing to the credit of Regina Maria Roche, is that facility which is still so para-mount a consideration today in novels that treat of sensibil-ity, or romance, or terror: a capacity to compel the reader to continue turning the page—even if in Roche's case at times with twinges of impatience. There can be little doubt that Regina Maria Roche was endued with that particular strength of literary creativity which quickly engages and, having engaged, inclines one with verve to keep going. Too often one palls at the over-lengthy elaborations of Ann Radcliffe. This is a shortcoming from which the author of *The Children of the Abbey* is exempt.

Clermont, shorter than *The Children of the Abbey*, is more firmly rooted in the gothic tradition, being set, not in Britain or Ireland, but in rural France during the declining years of the pre-Revolution *ancien régime*. It is a novel through which the tentacles of mystery writhe with a pervasive malevo-lence, though the reins that control them ever are held by an unshakeably secure authorial hand. At first blush, *Clermont* resembles *The Children of the Abbey* as a story that predomi-nantly treats of romantic sensibility. Madeline, who lives with her father, Clermont, in an obscure woodland cottage, early encounters the handsome de Sevignie. Passion is fast ignited, but a stop-start romance between the two is inter-rupted by de Sevignie's insistence on obstacles he is loath to explain. Madeline's father has known better times, and when a friend of his youth, Countess de Merville, arrives at his cottage after a mishap with her carriage, he is pleased to accede to her suggestion that she take and maintain his daughter in her château as a ward. During this period a warm friendship springs up between Madeline and Countess de Merville, and the assiduities of de Sevignie, never far away, continue to be pressed with bewildering intermittence. Thus far thus predictable, though, unlike in the earlier work, the backgrounds both of Madeline and de Sevignie are shrouded in mystery. In *Children of the Abbey*, Fitzalan's secret marriage and its consequences are early revealed as back story, while there never is much to bemuse about the origins of Lord Mortimer. Clermont's history has suffered at the hands both of tragedy and violence, and he and the countess are at pains to forbid Madeline ever inquiring into it.

More so than in *Children*, in *Clermont* depictions of atmosphere and landscape are plied with ladling regularity, thereby maintaining a uniform sombreness of tone, though even here one feels less imbued with consciousness of scenic grandeur than in the greatest productions of Ann Radcliffe. Most particularly is the area about château de Valdore (Countess de Merville's home), and the ruined monastery adjoining it, limned with sempiternal nocturnal bleakness. Owls and ravens wheel about, and there are many grim-weather days featuring heavy cloud and rain. The night of the death of the countess is the scene of a violent storm, which is portrayed with powerful effect. And her funeral procession yields no place to more famous authors of the gothic:

> "The solemn *requiem* chaunted by the monks, as they preceded the body, the glimmering light of the torches, carried by the servants, which as it fell in partial directions upon the old trees that canopied the garden walk through which they past to the valley,

produced a thousand quivering and grotesque shadows; the melancholy notes of the birds, who, deceived
by the light, started from their nests, and the low mur-
murs of the wind amongst the branches, altogether
produced an effect upon Madeline that wrought her
feelings up to agony."

For half its length *Clermont* dwells upon the juddering relationship between Madeline and de Sevignie and the increasingly grim hue of her experiences at château de Valdore. A
night assault on the countess in the chapel of the ruined
monastery—by a person obviously known to her, but whose
identity it is clear she is determined to conceal—which
leads to her death, is the only hint up to this point of aught
ominous or sinister. All changes, however, upon Madeline's
chance arrival at the château de Montmorenci, when returning to her father's house, and her encounter there with the
reclusive marquis. This sets in train a series of events, of a
complexity no less intricate than mind-boggling, which after
many travails in the closing pages puts all to rights. It is from
this point that the tortuous and tragic story of Clermont
comes to be revealed.

But not all at once. Firstly, Clermont recounts the
bare story of his childhood residence with the parents of
Countess de Merville, the Valdores. Then he passes a manu-
script penned by his long-dead mother to Madeline to read.
In this, Clermont's mother, another Madeline, tells the tale
of the betrayal that destroyed her life. Next, Clermont
resumes his own narrative, which summarily concludes with
the deaths of his wife, Madeline's mother, and his brother.
Madeline feels cause to dread from the tale's truncated con-
clusion that all that should have been, has not yet been told.
After she and her father, by the marquis's invitation, arrive
at the château de Montmorenci, ghostly manifestations, à

la *Udolpho*, begin to occur. Anguished groans heard from a room which a man believed murdered once occupied, a hand appearing from behind a tapestry to indict her father with concealed crime. Clermont recounts his life story to the marquis, but omits making reference to a brother. And last, when the novel's most consummate villain appears on the scene, his machinations extort a confession out of Clermont which shows a yet more twisted and convoluted skein than any heretofore imagined. But even that is not the complete picture, the final and confused details of which emerge only in the concluding chapter. Credibility falls casualty to contrivance of narrative, but the contrivance is surely worked and our author never stumbles.

If *Clermont* suffers in reputation from coming four years after *The Mysteries of Udolpho*, and showing unmistakeable signs of deference to the worn treads of a gothic tradition that, having reached its summit, was soon to drift into decline, there are also elements to Regina Roche's novel which cast their gaze forward and anticipate traits of Ireland's later great master of the ghostly tale, J. S. Le Fanu. While what turns out to have been the death watch for Countess de Merville is in train, the only authentic ghostly tale in the entire novel is related in an exchange between two of the countess's servants, Agatha and Floretta, with Madeline a reluctant, uneasy auditor. Cleverly, the story that each one recounts to the other portends the dark and dreadful secret which Clermont has long concealed. One is reminded, in embryo, of the hiding of Le Fanu's powerful tale "Madam Crowl's Ghost" as a sub-story in "An Adventure in the Life of Miss Laura Mildmay"; similarly of that author's "Ghost Stories of the Tiled House" tucked away like goblin offspring in *The House by the Churchyard*.

When Madeline is beguiled into fleeing to Paris out of the dubious security of château de Montmorenci, from the moment of her arrival in the disagreeable, weed-and-rub-bish-cluttered residence of Madame Fleury we are straight into the territory of the climax of *Uncle Silas*. A supposed flight to the bosom of safety leads one instead into con-cealed jaws of peril, or—as in the case of Lady Dunreath's expected passage to Paris in *Children of the Abbey*, which ends with her returned as a prisoner to the abbey—right back amid the dangers we had hoped to escape. And, when we meet the drugged shape of Clermont (by this stage believed by his daughter to be safe away in an Alpine hideout) lying prone in a room of Madame Fleury's bodeful abode—"thin, ghastly, to all appearance dead"—it is not too vast a stretch of fancy to perceive in prospect the moribund, sup-posed deceased shape of Richard Beckett as decked out for burial alive in Le Fanu's mystery novella "The Room in the Dragon Volant".

There is risk in pressing too hard a case to descry fore-shadowings from Roche to Le Fanu. Callisthenics of the intel-lect or imagination are no sound route to accurate analysis. Even so, sure it is that the two successive gothic progenies of Regina Maria Roche occupy roles more vital than of imitators of Ann Radcliffe or "Radcliffe lite". The Irish author may not emulate her famous counterpart in terms of attainment to the Edmund Burke aesthetic of rendered sublime, but there are other elements wherein merit lies—talent to compel a reader to keep reading is no negligible instance of one.

In places, Roche's gothic novels display traces of deeper purpose than that of simple titillation or the unending *déroule-ment* of suspense. In *Children*, when Amanda to all appear-ances has given up hope of ever winning Mortimer, and, in an effort to wrest back his inheritance for her brother, is driven, by sundry devices, to wander the streets of London destitute and homeless, the author shows, with harrowing vividness, how frighteningly close repeated misfortune can bring one to the brink of degradation. Amanda is rescued from her perils by an earlier admirer, who yet requires evidence to assure him that his one-time beloved has not sunk to become a woman of the streets. Stretching over a penumbra of mystery and machination in *Clermont*, is the awesome awful spectre of the crime of fratricide and the far-too-facile means by which a family can be brought to ruin by a moment's burst of violent passion deceitfully induced.

From strengths such as these it would be a mistake to infer that *Clermont*'s being listed among Isabella Thorpe's "horrid" novels in *Northanger Abbey* is aimed as a slur by Jane Austen against the Irish author of romance. There may well indeed be more sober and retrospectively respectful elements in play. The use of the surname of Sir Charles Bingley, Amanda Fitzalan's understudy stalwart in *Children of the Abbey*, for a key character in Austen's *Pride and Prejudice* shows more of homage perhaps than haughty dismissal. And what are we to make of the kinship between Lafroy and Lefroy? The former is a villainous servant of the marquis de Montmorenci, who all but succeeds in destroying Madeline and her father in *Clermont*. The latter, as Tom Lefroy, was a young lawyer admirer of Jane Austen in the 1790s, a man whom she never came to marry, but who himself was many years later a lord chief justice in one of Ireland's higher courts. True, Lefroy is less likely a name for an Irish superior court judge than is Lafroy for a rascally French servant. Still, one is driven to wonder whether Regina Maria Roche knew somewhat more than she revealed, and whether Jane Austen in turn was not quite averse to duly tipping the cap of acknowledgement.

Leaner and casting a razor-sharp shadow back to the more succinct sepulchral offerings of *The Castle of Otranto* and Clara Reeve's *The Old English Baron* of 1778, is Stephen Cullen's 1794 production *The Haunted Priory; or, The Fortunes of the House of Rayo*. Of this author, whose *The Haunted Priory* can claim to be the first gothic novel set in medieval Spain, little seems to be known; and—other than on the basis of his second (and final) gothic offering, *The Castle of Inchvally: A Tale—Alas! Too True*, sited mainly in Ireland and which involves an Irish cast of characters—the best evidence to support a claim to Irishness resides in his name, which suggests that either he or his progenitors hailed, like Regina Maria Roche, from south-east Leinster.

In large part a historical novel—or one substantially prompted by vicissitudes of history, akin to *Longsword*—Cullen's *The Haunted Priory* details the plummet and remarkable restoration of the fortunes of the war baron de Rayo, in tandem with the trials that beset his kinsman Isidor de Haro. De Rayo is an equivocal personality: a good man and a loyal man, but filled with a fervour for right and justice that is set by military implacability into a sometime-seeming hardness, and infused with colourful philosophic apothegms which form a filigree screen for the stridently felt sentiments of this novel's obscure author. The fulcrum for ghostly abetment lies in the mysterious disappearance of the baron's daughter Maria, with her husband Henrico Gonsalvo and their infant son Alphonso, in the course of a war campaign when the de Rayo family's loyalty to the reigning king of Spain is called in question. Flung into prison, the baron has frequent dream visitations from his son, who shows "a ghastly wound on his head" that "discovered his brains" and entreats him to seek his lost child. Released after the death of the tyrant king, de Rayo's intense unwearying searches throw him on the comradeship of the more even-tempered de Haro, whose son, also Alphonso, the baron befriends. It is through this Alphonso that the novel's authentic supernatural machinery is put in harness to actuate the process by which harrowing discovery is made and retribution meted to the guilty. A ghostly manifestation occurs near the end of volume one of this slim two-volume *oeuvre*, which by any standard is impressive—casting into shadow by comparison the absurd gigantism of *The Castle of Otranto*'s whimsical appearances and the muted groaning under floorboards which characterises the gothic high point of *The Old English Baron*. On Christmas night, in a remote and rugged rural setting deftly sketched with far-from-overdone touches of Edmund Burke's sublime, Alphonso is led to an uncannily lit abbey, where a spectral choir is singing to the tune of a thunderous organ, a place during daylight found empty and abandoned; meets a huge armour-clad figure that goads him forward yet ever eludes his efforts to keep pace with it; and follows a supernatural figure "rendered visible by a lambent flame that played about it", its long hair "entangled with clotted gore", which vanishes through a wall that traps the tip of Alphonso's sword thrust frantically in its wake.

Volume two elaborates the machinations of the marquis de Punalada and of his abbot collaborator whose life is lasting testament to "what mischiefs may lurk beneath the monkish cowl". In a manner not unmindful of the determined band of avengers led by Van Helsing in Bram Stoker's *Dracula* a century later, so de Rayo, with the support of Isidor de Haro, and Alphonso, and the good priest Fr. Thomas, embarks on a series of supernaturally monitored incursions to the crypt of Vallesanto convent, where dark discoveries are made, of which the uncoffined corpses of a number of monks—"in various stages of dissolution, some mouldered to dust, some half consumed, and some in a more offensive state of putrefaction, lying on their backs, with crucifixes tied erect in their hands"—constitute not the most horrific finds in terms of murderous dastardliness in play. And of course, a noble lady of unsurpassed and impenetrable virtue is found immured in the vaults, and later also a half-starved hag who had undertaken a particular and pertinent *substitution* many years earlier!

Another staunch plot ingredient of the gothic makes no mean inroad into the activities of *The Haunted Priory*—incest. The marquis de Punalada's son lusts for his sister who is confined to a nunnery, and meets a bloody end when, striving by night to climb to her room, a rope-ladder goes awry with resultant tumble atop a spiked railing in the courtyard below; the released noble lady believes she sees in one of her rescuers the form of her murdered husband and discovers, eventually, her son; while Alphonso falls in love with a prim beauty whom he rescues from a would-be ravisher to incur the wrath of his father for desiring his own sister, only later to learn she is not such . . .

Stephen Cullen's *The Haunted Priory* makes fair claim to be the first gothic novel by an Irish author with an underpinning of the genuine supernatural. Its prime difficulty resides in the time when it was written—the mid-1790s—with *Otranto* and *The Old English Baron*, its obvious preceptors, by then the classic gothic progeny of a previous generation, while Radcliffe's *Udolpho* hit the presses the very same year, and Matthew Lewis's *The Monk*, also a gothic novel of authentic supernaturalism likewise set in a Spanish milieu, was to be the controversial hot offering of only the year after.

If *The Haunted Priory* shows that its author Stephen Cullen had taken tutelage from the gothic efforts of Horace Walpole and Clara Reeve, his longer, more densely-woven *The Castle of Inchvally: A Tale—Alas! Too True*, published in three volumes in 1796, displays that lessons had since been learned from the contrivances of Ann Radcliffe, if rather less from the theory of the sublime propounded by Edmund Burke. Of the story's overarching artifice, let naught be said than that Fr. Dominic O'Farrell's two little-encountered *confrères* at the Dominican friary in the demesne of Inchvally are of more than scant significance, and that the credulity even of educated papists at the time offers fertile soil for imposition. Supernatural fire plays a crucial part, in the spectacle of sulphur-stenching spirits that move about on skeletal limbs, to appear unexpectedly in a gallery corridor, bearing shapes "composed of fire of various tints", and emitting sounds in a voice "like that of a departed soul speaking from the cavity of a yawning grave", with blood-curdling laughter "of that terrific and malignant expression devils may be supposed to utter when pleased". Most crucially, Inchvally is a gothic novel about Ireland set in Ireland. It is a novel eloquent of passion and anger—at the abuses of law forced on the majority inhabitants of the island, and the mutual intolerance practised by ministers of the Catholic Church and the Church of Ireland. Characters give vent to feelings with a colourful rhetoric impossible not to be thought of as felt by its author: so that we find thunderous invective deployed against "vile heretics, plundering protestant peculators", who are believed prone to engage in "large draughts of reformation rancour", on one hand, and on the other, "the talismanic folly and fraud of churchmen" of the Roman faith, it being asserted that "if mankind were to make a fair calculation of their various ills in life . . . sure there would be none found such ruinous enemies to human happiness and human greatness as priests".

Inchvally Castle is one of the few estates of antiquity in Ireland that somehow survived in catholic hands. Richard Howard, its current owner, marries a protestant lady, for love, against the advice of religion and his relatives, and is made to rue it. Early on, we encounter the curse of ascetic-featured great-uncle Arthur, who has spent most of his life in Spain (and so has to be *told* of the numbing effect of the relaxation of the penal laws by Fr. O'Farrell), together with the fulminations of aunt Lissarda, "a priggish piece of fanaticism", who endows herself liberally with crucifixes, pixes, and various impedimenta of saintly statuary. As part of the marriage settlement with his wife's father, Richard has agreed that his sons will be brought up protestant, his daughters Catholic unless the heir is a daughter. His first child, a daughter Arabella, is baptised catholic by the indulgence of Howard's father-in-law in expectation of later male issue. His second, a son, accordingly is set to be baptised protestant—but on a night of intense ghostly activity the infant is spirited out of the castle despite doors being locked and gates barred. A stone coffin is found in a concealed room, which contains a human skeleton in whose hands is clasped a crucifix and a roll of parchment: this paper is discovered to contain a sinister (but from the reader unduly long withheld) "monition". The baby's father is unable to track him down, and his mother dies of grief a few years later. The Howards have enjoyed friendly relations with a nearby protestant family, that of Sir Clement Wilmot, a magistrate, which has blossomed out of a pre-marriage amity between the wives. The second son of the Wilmots, Charles, is a few months older than Arabella. Not long after Arabella Howard is born, the mothers form a wish that their offspring will one day marry each other. The fathers indulge the desire of their wives. As the children grow to maturity, infantine fondness between them ripens to love. However, following an illness that brings him near death, Richard Howard, now a widower, changes heart and sets his face against the troth he had once supported. He has become persuaded that his soul will be damned if he allows his daughter marry a "heretic". Much of the rest of the novel is concerned with the tribulation of the lovers and the tortuous but total unravelling of a whole heap of queer yet connected complications.

The discerning reader may feel that the virtues of Sir Clement Wilmot and his son Charles all but transcend the confines of human nature. On the obverse side, the heir to the title, Godfrey, is portrayed as possessing a black-heartedness and brutality that almost would incline one to question his parentage; with, not one, but *two*, attempted sexual assaults on Arabella Howard, each set at naught by happenstance violent intervention. Equally, Richard Howard's descent from decency to mulcted half-madness betimes strains at the leash of credibility. Even so—better it is suggested than Mrs. Radcliffe—Stephen Cullen succeeds in the creation of vivid and memorable characters, especially those of eccentric stripe. Of these, perhaps the most enduring is the elderly country physician, Jemmy Heartly, a tolerant catholic who loves his protestant neighbours, is unsparing of himself in attention to his duty to all and never takes a fee, whose friendships are always with young people rather than old, and among whose perennial amusements is the netting of partridge with the aim of conserving them to breed. Dr. Heartly is a constant throughout the book, but his match for brusque benignity and unorthodox life is met by Captain Miles Markham, whom we discover in volume three, a "benevolent misanthrope" whose colourful and curious history, and even more curious quirks of penetration, help bring all things to a happy end for those who deserve being made happy.

In particular, Cullen demonstrates an aptitude for energetic and confrontational dialogue—not an inevitable attribute of the typical gothic novel—especially evidenced on issues of religious toleration and personal probity: witness, for example, Richard Howard's indignant invective against "his aunt Lissarda continually croaking at his elbow" and her evil genius O'Farrell after the death of his wife; a scene of blistering broadside between Sir Clement Wilmot and the Church of Ireland bishop who defends an intemperate attack in a parson's sermon; and Dr. Heartly's doughty presentation to his once friend Richard Howard, at the close of volume two, of the dishonourable latterday error of his ways. It is hoped, too, in the illustrations offered that the reader will concur that Cullen is no mean practitioner in the apt and allusive use of language!

Even after the story is told one finds oneself returning to the characters and the theme. This theme is that of a decent people—the Irish—subdued, without remission, by the injustice of a religion not their own, and the fanatical intolerance of that which is, the combination abetted by the covin of a government whose objective is to cow. Indeed, in the early exchange between Fr. O'Farrell and great-uncle Arthur, one of the *drawbacks* adumbrated by the priest in the relaxing of the penal laws is that the process has blunted national sense of grievance, so that "the natural milky disposition of the Irish gradually softened their hearts into forgiveness", with the undesired result that "the spirit of hatred" between catholics and protestants would disperse "without which they would soon coalesce, and pay no more than reasonable homage to either Papal or British government, which I am sorry to foresee will one day be the case."

Predictive language—but it has taken more than two centuries to bring this eventuality about, and even still not fully!

Inevitably and regrettably, *The Castle of Inchvally* suffers by comparison with the more tightly written and much better known *Castle Rackrent* by Maria Edgeworth published four years later. Yet for all the rackety verisimilitude with which this short *début* novel points up a rude and rough style of Irish country living that even by 1800 was a memory tending to fade, and its occasional shadow-glances at folk ghostliness, *Castle Rackrent* is not, nor could ever be truly reckoned to be, a gothic novel.

By the first decade of the nineteenth century, the gothic novel had strayed well past the peak of its best prowess and was in danger of descending into a treadmill of potboilers. Among much of the dross whipped up in that turbulent time, one novel stands out unique for invention and a welcome depth of intensity. To boot, the name ascribed its author set him apart beyond shadow of doubt as being Irish. This was *Fatal Revenge; or, The Family of Montorio* by Dennis Jasper Murphy. Alone of all of the writers of Irish gothic fiction considered so far, this one in time would win lasting renown, but under that name which was truly his own— Charles Robert Maturin.

ॐ

In our next instalment we will consider the pinnacle reached by the gothic novel in Ireland.

The Long Reach of Green Shadows: Ray Bradbury's Memories of Ireland

Steve Gronert Ellerhoff

"What was I? I was a bag of potatoes that grew up in Ireland finally."

– *Ray Bradbury*

Ray Bradbury (1920-2012) was a connoisseur of nostalgia, an artist who drew again and again from his own longed-for past. His Orphean gaze often looked over shoulder to his Illinois childhood, culminating in cycles of Midwestern stories written from an agreeable adulthood exile in Southern California. *Dandelion Wine* (1957), his third novel, brings together tales about Douglas Spalding of Green Town, both boy and community bearing autobiographical dimensions. Green Town stood in for his hometown of Waukegan, Illinois, while Douglas was a fictionalised composite of Bradbury's childhood self: his middle name was Douglas, while Spaulding had been his father's and grandfather's middle name. As Bradbury lived and experienced life, this alter ego perennially appeared in his short fiction, inspired so often by actual events. So when Ray Bradbury was invited to spend six months in Ireland adapting Herman Melville's *Moby-Dick* for the silver screen, Douglas Spalding was sure to follow.

The man who insisted the young screenwriter come to Ireland, film director John Huston, was renting a Georgian country house in County Kildare called Courtown and wanted the writer working nearby. So in early October 1953,

Bradbury, his wife Maggie, their two daughters, and a nanny arrived in Dún Laoghaire from the UK by ferry. Huston put them up at the Royal Hibernian Hotel on Dawson Street in Dublin and Bradbury set to work, adapting Melville's whaling epic at the behest of the man famous for directing *The Maltese Falcon* (1941). Many nights were spent being driven by cab to Courtown to review his progress with Huston, who vacillated between praising and belittling the writer, whose sensitivities, in turn, gave way to anxieties. The Irish winter and professional pressures proved a toxic combination. "I was suicidal," Bradbury said, "for the first time in my life" (Weller, *Chronicles* 222). On 1 February 1954, he sent his family to Sicily so they might find some relaxation following the stress; Bradbury stayed on alone to do battle with the white whale. During this time he revised the final two-thirds of his screenplay, while his relationship with Huston deteriorated beyond true reconciliation. He left Ireland at the beginning of April from the very same point of entry, Dún Laoghaire Port, never to return to Ireland.

Despite the grief and depression, Bradbury would, as he did with his childhood and trips to Mexico, cultivate nostalgia for Ireland. Biographer Sam Weller writes that "as painful as many of the memories were, there was something undeniably romantic about the loneliness he had felt there" (239). Bradbury recalled this tug in 2009 when introducing a performance of one of his Irish plays, *Falling Upward*: "When I got home a voice said in my mind, 'Ray, darling.' I said, 'Who's that?' He said, 'It's your cab driver that drove you out along the Liffey three days a week to meet with John Huston. Do you remember that?' I said, 'Yes.' He said, 'Would you mind puttin' it down?' " (ForrestJBradbury). "The First Night of Lent", the first fictional shaping of his Irish experiences, was published in the March 1956 issue of *Playboy*, two years after he left. More Irish stories would follow over the next thirty-five years, culminating with his eighth novel, *Green Shadows, White Whale* (1992).

Bradbury fraternally twinned his title to screenwriter Peter Viertel's *roman à clef White Hunter, Black Heart* (1953). Written shortly after his adaptation of C. S. Forester's *The African Queen* (also for Huston) Viertel's novel depicts a screenwriter struggling with the fictional film director "John Wilson", who nearly sabotages his own film with an obsession for hunting elephants. *Green Shadows, White Whale*, pieced together nearly forty years after Viertel's book, similarly depicts a screenwriter struggling to adapt a classic work of literature for an obsessed director—but this time John Huston is named outright. Bradbury quilted his novel from many, but not all, of the Irish stories written over three decades, adding material as needed to pattern his own semi-autobiographical account. Of the twelve previously published stories used for the novel, nine debuted in magazines before 1970, setting composition of much of the book's content well before its publication in 1992. "The Hunt Wedding", an essay that appeared in *The American Way* (May 1992), is also incorporated. Three of the stories were published as one-act plays in *The Anthem Sprinters & Other Antics* (Dial Press 1963), and in 1988 Bradbury pieced two of these one-acts together to produce the play *Falling Upward*. Also worth noting is the fact that leading up to the novel, Bradbury adapted several of the Irish stories for his television series, *The Ray Bradbury Theater*, which ran from 1985 to 1992. There were, however, two works that fall within Bradbury's Irish fiction that were not incorporated into the novel: the story "The Better Part of Wisdom" (1976) and the one-act "A Clear View of an Irish Mist" (1963). Their exclusion indicates that *Green Shadows* is more than just a cut-and-paste effort.

When Bradbury's Irish stories were initially published, his alter ego, Douglas, was sometimes named as the screenwriter who has arrived in Dublin to work on a film. "Douglas" narrates "The First Night of Lent" (1956), "The Anthem Sprinters" (1963), and "Banshee" (1984, as Douglas Rogers). Though not identified by name, it can be assumed that Douglas also narrates "A Wild Night in Galway" (1959), "The Beggar on the O'Connell Bridge" (1961), "Getting Through Sunday Somehow" (1962), and "McGilahee's Brat" (1970). When these stories appeared in *Green Shadows*, there is no mention of Douglas—or the name Ray Bradbury. But because John Huston is explicitly named as the director, clearly it is Bradbury himself who is the narrator. Despite this, the narrator remains unnamed—but occasionally allows Huston to call him "H. G.", short for H. G. Wells. Later, a fictional former flame, Nora (Barnacle perhaps?), calls him William, Willy, and Will, flattering him with a pet name—an allusion to Shakespeare. (In the original short story, "The Haunting of the New" (1969), he is simply Charles, Charlie, or Chuck.) For some reason Bradbury remains reluctant to identify himself fully in the text, even though the dust jacket blurb on the first edition underlines his biographical connection to Ireland and the story therein.

Perhaps this distancing comes down to the mechanics of the fiction-infused memoir. While Bradbury is happy to admit that the novel is inspired by actual events (he even names Huston's fourth wife Ricki) he has all but excised his own family from the Irish experience. Bradbury depicts his time on the island as spent alone, even though his wife, daughters, and their nanny were actually with him for four of the six months. Also absent from the novel are Huston's children, Anjelica and Tony. We can speculate any number of reasons for these choices: from Bradbury protecting the innocent to the possibility that populating a narrative with family members brings further complications. The only certainty is that when fusing his life and prior fiction into the novel Bradbury left certain people out of the story, much the same way he cut fire-worshipping Fedallah from *Moby-Dick* when writing his screenplay. The familial exclusion has a profound effect in particular on chapter thirteen, revised from "The Beggar on the O'Connell Bridge". When initially published in *The Saturday Evening Post* (14 January 1961), the narrator's wife plays his foil; in *Green Shadows*, the wife is simply replaced, often with dialogue intact, by the saturnine Huston.

In his final years, Bradbury often credited his experiences in Ireland as having established him as a financially secure writer with a respected reputation. Whereas Viertel rushed to express in his own novel the trauma of working with John Huston, Bradbury waited decades, until he was on the other side of adulthood, to draw the experiences together. Biographer and scholar Jon R. Eller has said that the novel "offers a balanced view of events, tempered by the passage of time" (55). The screenwriting job forms the basis of his narrator's focus, though it often slips out of the narrative as episodic events emerge. While Huston is cast as Ahab to Bradbury's Starbuck, Ireland and myriad Irish characters repeatedly interrupt their self-imposed and often frustrating work together. This is not to say Ireland and the Irish are used merely as comic relief, but there is plenty of comedy, and the narrator often takes relief in the company of these characters. And the question they repeatedly pose to the screenwriter is asked upfront in the book's opening scene by a customs inspector in Dún Laoghaire: "Your reason for being in Ireland?"

"Reason has nothing to do with it," he answers (2). After all, there is no tie to *Moby-Dick* that would make adapting it on Irish soil pertinent. Indeed, these Americans are in Ireland simply because they can be. In Melville's novel, Ishmael asks, "What to that redoubted harpooner, John Bull, is poor Ireland, but a Fast-Fish?" (310). According to whaling rules, "A Fast-Fish belongs to the party fast to it" (308). John Bull stands in for England in Ishmael's statement, but the same could be said about John Huston. Huston's choice of Ireland was simply because he felt entitled to it. Bradbury offers fox-hunts and horse riding as Huston's main draw to the island, not the people, the culture, the history, or even the typical American lure of ancestry. There is not a single good reason for the narrator to be brought far from his home in Southern California, the capital of American film-making and where screenwriting is an established industry. Huston's irrational choice of work setting effectively makes every scene and every encounter Bradbury's narrator has with Ireland twinkle with serendipity.

For Bradbury, who proudly sentimentalised whatever he loved, Ireland receives his signature nostalgic treatment. Stereotypes of the land and people abound. Ireland is green: "Not just one ordinary sort of green, but every shade and variation. Even the shadows were green" (1). Rain abounds, as does fog, the weather played up in a typical fashion. But where many narratives of a stranger in a known land will use local landmarks to excess, *Green Shadows* remains innocent of that literary misdemeanor. Dublin is largely limited to Grafton Street, St. Stephen's Green, and the O'Connell Bridge. When dealing with Huston, the setting typically shifts to the grounds of Courtown in Co. Kildare; and when recovering from the stress caused by the director, to Heeber Finn's Pub in Kilcock. There are no side-trips to kiss the Blarney Stone, no sheep-gaze at Tara, and no walks along the Giant's Causeway in the North. *Green Shadows* does not stand as a traditional travel narrative, and while the narrator is conscious of his own naiveté—" 'Kind to Dogs' is writ on my brow," he claims (90)—this is not *The Innocents Abroad*.

"The greatest temptation for a writer in dealing with the Irish," wrote Irish critic Bruce Cook in his 1966 article "Ray

Bradbury and the Irish", "is to be taken in by their quaint-ness" (225). Coming from the Midwest, the region most stereotypically equated with quaintness in the United States, Bradbury plays up this quality in the Irish while also playing it up in his narrator. It is difficult to fault him with this tendency when he so readily makes it a foundational aspect of his alter ego. His folksy, hail-fellow-well-met manner harmonises with the many Irish characters, and forms an in-road to their lives. And while no intimate connections are made, friendliness meets friendliness and casual acquaintances are plentiful.

Cab driver Nick and publican Heeber Finn receive the most attention. Finn even takes over narration in chapters twelve and eighteen, telling tales previously published as "The Terrible Conflagration Up at the Place" (1969) and "One for His Lordship, and One for the Road!" (1985); and again in chapter twenty-six when he relates a story about George Bernard Shaw visiting his pub. But these are the only instances during which the narrator yields to an Irish character, showing Bradbury's effort to represent a sus-tained Irish voice. Thankfully he does not attempt to ren-der brogue through dialectical spelling, apart from the odd "Jaisus", and this is much to Bradbury's credit. And while the characters' speech may not always ring true to an Irish reader, it can hardly offend.

The pub stories are often humorous, focusing on play-ful conflicts between locals and gentry, represented here as Lord Kilgotten. One of Finn's tales recounts an episode from the revolution where their intention to burn down the lord's house is foiled by Kilgotten's gentle appeal that they spare his artwork, which all appreciate. In the another story, old Kilgotten has died, his departure "like the Normans' rowing back to France or the damned Brits pulling out of Bombay" (129), and his intention to take his wine collection to the grave with him is circumvented by a crowd of thirsty villagers all too happy to make sure that his last wish come true. "And bless this wine, which may circumnavigate along the way, but finally wind up where it should be going," they solemnly swear. "And if today and tonight won't do, and all the stuff not drunk, bless us as we return each night until the deed is done and the soul of the wine's at rest" (139). These tales are not so much parody of Ireland's fight for independence as they are Bradbury's pastiche of the stories he heard told in pubs by the people he met.

Another demographic that receives attention is the urban poor of Dublin, beggars being central in two distinct episodes. Bradbury, a survivor of the Great Depression, was not ignorant of hardship. His father was out of work for long periods during his childhood and lack of money dictated that the suit he wore to high school graduation came from an uncle who had been shot dead wearing it. But in the early fifties he was also getting to know American prosperity, making his living as a writer in the post-war years. His anxieties about money and the potential lack of it are present in his fixation on Irish beggars. In the first episode he resolves to help a blind concertina-player, often seen on the O'Connell Bridge, by buying him a cap to keep his head dry, only to discover the man committed suicide the day before by jumping into the Liffey. In another chapter, Dublin is covered by rare snow falls, and the narrator, standing outside the Royal Hibernian Hotel where he is staying, looks up at the lit windows wondering what it is like inside. This is his private, conscious attempt to put himself in the beggar's place. Later in the novel, he interacts with some beggars he recognises from his first trip to Ireland, fifteen years in the past. The catch is that the woman's infant has not grown in all that time. The narrator discovers that the babe is actually her dwarf brother. The narrator's attitude to the beggars this go around, after first unmasking the ruse, is to adopt a conspiratorial stance, promising to keep their secret and not write about it for thirty years. The siblings' hope is to save enough money to emigrate to New York, a Tír na nÓg wish the narrator supports. And so Bradbury's Dublin is home to beggars both despondent and hopeful. Their presence provides a contrast to the bored, almost aristocratic wealth displayed by Huston and his acquaintances among the fox-hunting class.

Bradbury's summation of the Irish people in the end is based on observations not of a Hibernophile, but of a working visitor. Finn asks him, before his departure and the close of the novel, "On the Irish now. Have you crossed our T's and dotted our I's? How would you best describe . . . ?" (269). The narrator's insight, for what it is worth, comes down to his appreciation for the people's imagination:

" 'Imagination,' I went on. 'Great God, everything's wrong. Where are you? On a flyspeck isle nine thousand miles north of nowhere!! What wealth is there? None! What natural resources? Only one: the resourceful genius, the golden mind, of everyone I've met! The mind that looks out the eyes, the words that roll off the tongue in response to events no bigger than the eye of a needle! From so little you glean so much; squeeze the last ounce of life from a flower with one petal, a night with no stars, a day with no sun, a theater haunted by old films, a bump on the head that in America would have been treated with a Band-Aid. Here and everywhere in Ireland, it goes on. Someone picks up a string, someone else ties a knot in it, a third one adds a bow, and by morn you've got a rug on the floor, a drape at the window, a harp-thread tapestry singing on the wall, all starting from that string! The Church puts her on her knees, the weather drowns her, politics all but buries her . . . but

> Ireland still sprints for that far exit. And do you know,
> by God, I think she'll *make* it!' " (269-70)

A portion of his declaration echoes Shaw from Finn's earlier story: "The Irish. From so little they glean so much: squeeze the last ounce of joy from a flower with no petals, a night with no stars, a day with no sun" (197). And while his narrator's exposure to Shaw in the novel amounts to what Finn has told him, Bradbury actually attended a performance of Shaw's play *St. Joan* while living in Dublin. That production marked the beginning of his love for Shaw, which only intensified as he aged. In 1976 he even published a tribute, "G.B.S.—Mark V", the story of a lonesome astronaut who befriends the robotic George Bernard Shaw installed on his rocket. And of Shaw's collected play prefaces, Bradbury in his eighth decade would say, "That book is my bible" (Weller, *Listen* 162). Shaw was his favourite writer in the second half of his life, making it deliberate that the narrator in *Green Shadows* should in the end turn to Shaw-*via*-Finn in his attempt to understand the Irish.

The men at the pub do not react to his summation of them. They do not stand or see him out as he leaves for good, making for a most casual farewell. There is no Lion, Tin Woodsman, or Scarecrow to embrace, the many acquaintances he made remain just that: acquaintances. The novel is dedicated in part "to the memory of Heeber Finn, Nick (Mike) my taxi driver, and all the boyos in the pub . . . " Memory of his cab driver spurred Bradbury to write his first Irish tale and it is to memory that he offered *Green Shadows, White Whale* nearly forty years later. Scholars Jonathan R. Eller and William F. Touponce believe "Bradbury's Irish ultimately turns out to be a reflection of his own concerns . . . about affirming the life of the imagination even in the presence of overwhelming negativity" (426). It is also his way of giving thanks to Ireland for providing the ground upon which he crossed the threshold into his own maturity.

Works Cited

Bradbury, Ray. *Green Shadows, White Whale*. New York: Alfred A. Knopf, 1992.

Cook, Bruce. "Ray Bradbury and the Irish". *Catholic World* 200 (1965): 224-30.

Eller, Jonathan R. "Adapting Melville for the Screen". *The New Ray Bradbury Review* 1 (2008): 35-60.

Eller, Jonathan R. and William F. Touponce. *Ray Bradbury: The Life of Fiction*. Kent: Kent State University, 2004.

ForrestJBradbury. "Ray Bradbury's Falling Upward— 90228". *YouTube*. YouTube, 3 Mar. 2009. 18 Nov. 2012.

Melville, Herman. *Moby-Dick*. New York: Norton, 2002.

Weller, Sam. *The Bradbury Chronicles: The Life of Ray Bradbury*. New York: Harper Perennial, 2005.

Weller, Sam. *Listen to the Echoes: The Ray Bradbury Interviews*. Brooklyn: Melville House, 2010.

Lord Dunsany 1878-1957:
Portrait of a Collector

Nicola Gordon Bowe

*"Most men collect something, and will know how a collection
illuminates leisure almost adding a purpose to life . . . a collection is such a satisfying thing."*

- Lord Dunsany, *Patches of Sunlight (1938)*[1]

Edward John Moreton Drax Plunkett, 18th Baron Dunsany,
writer, cricketer and chess champion, began by collecting
butterflies and moths when he was a small boy exploring
the "chalk hills and valleys and old black yew-trees", the surrounding woods "full of mystery", and the hedgerows, fields
and banks of wildflowers of the rolling North Kent landscape around his mother's beloved house, Dunstall Priory,
near Shoreham; later came stamps and then fossils (particularly uncut opals). One of his earliest memories of a house
filled with exotic, "strange things with a kind of magic about
them"[2] was "of a frog band in Dresden china that used to
be on brackets on a wall of the drawing room"; this led him
to notice later "that anyone's love of a house seems in the
course of years to enter the very walls of it and to shine
back from them at other generations". In subsequent years,
his collecting yen would extend to the myriad trophies he
unstoppably shot at home and abroad, and to a little-doc-
umented range of first-rate Arts and Crafts book bindings
and illustrations, furniture and pottery which complemented

the Billiard Room he commissioned from George Jack after he had brought his young English bride back to his ancestral castle in Ireland.[3]

Although Lord Dunsany was born in London in 1878, and raised there, at Dunstall and in his father's Gloucestershire constituency, the focus of this article is the ancient castle at Dunsany in County Meath, where his ancestors had lived more or less continuously since 1190. He would later write:

> "Of the date I can tell you nothing accurate. It was built by a forbear of ours who was a historical character, but it is just about that time that the history of Ireland begins to be fabulous; so that it is truer to tell you merely that the house was very old. Of the period of its furniture and its fixtures I can tell you at once: it was no period at all. As chairs and such things wore out they were replaced in different generations, and the only thing that they all had in common was that they were all bought by the same family. There is a right and a wrong place for antiquity; it is right in walls, wrong in carpets; wrong too in curtains and wall-paper and hearth-rugs. We had antiquity everywhere".[4]

His earliest schoolboy memory of visiting it with his father was in 1889, shortly before his grandfather died, where he remembered "tall bearded men at work about the place", and being taught to shoot by the gamekeeper. During prep school and Eton holidays, he revelled in vigourous outdoor pursuits, especially cricket, intrepid boating expeditions, shooting, and riding; when he not out exploring the "heathery wildernesses" of the untamed bog and the open countryside, he was introduced by his Aunt Mary Ponsonby to the literary wonders of William Morris's *Earthly Paradise* and to Kipling. He discovered Tennyson and began writing poems, expressing "my wish to be in Ireland, walking the bogs with my gun".[5] All the while, his eye was scanning the landscape, musing on its awesome beauties and anomalies:

> "Without a sense of mystery a man may be a scientist, a mathematician or many other things, but he cannot be a poet, for he has no land to travel in, no pasture on which to graze Pegasus, the frontier of the man-of-the-world lying just outside the edge of the lands of wonder."[6]

At Sandhurst, he co-authored his first story with Lord Howard de Walden, poet, polymath and "lavish patron of the arts" who shared his "preoccupation with mystery and romance" and would, like Dunsany, commission legendary masterpieces of design from their similarly imaginative older colleague, the illustrator Sidney Sime.[7] In 1899, his brilliant but erratic father was buried in the vault of the 500 year old ruined church at Dunsany and he set off, first for Gibraltar with the Coldstream Guards. There he was enchanted by the beauty of the sea and began to yearn for the "sunlight and dust and . . . desert lands" of the East; instead he had to make do with the dramatic sunsets of the South African veldt during service in the Boer War. What remained in his memory was decidedly unmilitary: meeting his hero Kipling, and his imagination continually conjuring up poems he as yet lacked the craftsmanship to record.

In 1901, Dunsany left the army, aged 23, tall, dashing, unconventional in dress[8] and behaviour, and relieved to be able to resume hunting, riding, shooting, and walking great distances wherever he happened to be.[9] Dunsany Castle, with its 14,000 acres, was being looked after by his uncle and trustee, the Rt. Hon. Horace Plunkett, politician, farmer, and an eminent figure in the Celtic Revival for his enlightened agricultural and co-operative reforms. Plunkett had already noticed his nephew had inherited "his father's brilliant imagination";[10] aged eighteen, he could "draw a nightmare", and could "write simple and rather musical English".[11] Horace Plunkett had been reared at Dunsany, "almost under the shadow of the Hill of Tara" where "we came under the spell which the spirit of the Celt used to weave round the offspring of the sternest of Irish invaders, making them more Irish than the Irish themselves".[12] Influenced by the Utopian socialist theories of Ruskin and Arnold Toynbee at Oxford, Plunkett had inaugurated a pioneering model co-operative store for his father's tenants to sell their produce. In 1894, he founded the enlightened Irish Agricultural Organisation Society, started up its weekly paper, *The Irish Homestead*, in 1895, met W.B. Yeats through Lady Gregory in 1896 and, in 1897, "conspired successfully" to engage the poet, painter, writer, nationalist, and Theosophist, George "Æ" Russell, to apply his visionary fervour, disingenuous charm, and teaching skills to the demoralised rural congested districts of Ireland.[13] Plunkett and his practical, apolitical cooperative scheme to regenerate autonomous Irish industries "soon became a focal point for Irish writers"[14] and those who supported the similarly revivalist Gaelic League. In 1897, *The Celtic Christmas*, a supplement of *The Irish Homestead*, became the first periodical to extend the paper's home industries programme into a visually attractive synthesis of evocative contributions from young contemporary writers and artists;[15] these included W.B. Yeats, Jack B. Yeats, Douglas Hyde, Standish O'Grady, Sarah Purser, Rosamond Praeger, Pamela Colman Smith, Æ, and Beatrice Elvery, each eminent in the Irish Arts and Crafts movement.

It should be remembered that "the Dunsanys belonged to the upper strata of Anglo-Irish society consisting of the major Irish landlords, most of whom owned houses in

London and often estates in England. They frequently inter-
married with their English counterparts and lived as much
in one country as the other".[16] During the 1903 London
summer season, while broaching a new political career, Lord
Dunsany met Lady Beatrice Villiers, a daughter of the Earl
and Countess of Jersey, who lived in eighteenth century
architectural splendour at Robert Adam's Osterley Park in
Middlesex and at Middleton Park in Oxfordshire. The following July, they became engaged and, in September 1904, married. His new wife's active interest encouraged him to write
in earnest, "guided . . . by two lights that do not seem very
often to shine together, poetry and humour".[17] He did make
drawings for the writings, somewhat biblical in tone, that he
gathered together into a book, "but had the sense to realise
that far better illustrations might be found". There were only
two men he felt could illustrate it, Gustave Doré, who was
dead, and Sidney Sime: "This remarkable man consented to
do me eight illustrations", which he was "left to do exactly as
he liked". Dunsany subsequently wrote he had "never seen a
black-and-white artist with a more stupendous imagination.
I think he is greater than Beardsley, and I do not know anyone now living who can bring such scenes of wonder down
upon paper with lamp-black and Indian ink".[18] A sketch
"done with an ordinary pen on a bit of paper the size of a
playing-card" was so suggestive that it could inspire Dunsany
to write a whole story. Thus, his debut collection, *The Gods of
Pegāna*, published by Elkin Mathews in 1905 and illustrated by
Sime, began a lifelong partnership between two kindred spirits, which would result in ten illustrated books over the next
thirty years.[19] Sometimes, as in *The Book of Wonder* (1912), the
pictures, "the very sources of wonder", inspired the stories.[20]

When Lady Dunsany arrived at the Castle, she found a
run-down bachelor establishment which "needed modern-
ising and improving", particularly in view of the comfort

to which she was accustomed. Meanwhile, Sir Horace had moved out of the Castle and commissioned a new house from the Swedish/English Arts Craft architect W.D. Caröe: Kilteragh was fan-shaped, white and harled with a monumental hinged door, leaded windows and outdoor sleeping porch south of Dublin, between the sea and the Dublin mountains. By 1906 it was ready for Æ's shimmering murals depicting Celtic heroes "on pale magic shores and blue-green seas", Sir Horace's renowned library, and a flow of distinguished guests. Filled with light, "it became a centre of Irish life. Every one interesting or interested who visited Ireland was entertained there."[21] The Dunsanys were fortunate to return to Ireland during this patriotic, National Romantic "renaissance in Irish cultural life", resulting in a revival of the "cooperation between the practical men and the dreamers"[22] not seen in Ireland since the golden Early Christian and Georgian periods. Kilteragh may well have inspired the Dunsanys, a few years later, to commission George Jack to build on "a billiard-room with two bedrooms and a bathroom above it which they fitted out with specially designed arty-crafty furniture. Dunsany bought anything that took his fancy at an exhibition, generally the work of a contemporary craftsman or living artist."[23]

Lord Dunsany enjoyed good craftsmanship, perhaps as an aspect of the "indebtedness of our spirits to Mother Earth"[24] that he instinctively felt. This led him to collect illustrated books and bindings, sometimes as receptacles for his own writings;[25] one of the most striking bindings, for his story "The Haunting of Whitebeams", is in morocco onlaid with whitebeam leaves and berries. These he would begin by dictating to his wife, then write out in a boldly flamboyant hand, picking out colours from a basket of pencils, before entrusting his words to purple ink. These he inscribed with a goose quill pen, whose bearer he had shot and whose quill he had carefully seasoned and sharpened. Sometimes he wrote between covers embroidered by his wife or other (unrecorded) skilled needlewomen;[26] sometimes between illuminated, gilded, or painted parchment covers, some decorated in the Italian Gothic manner advocated by Ruskin. He also commissioned leather tooled bindings, "workmanlike as well as artistic",[27] from Douglas Cockerell and his Central School of Arts and Crafts class in London, and another which appears to be by Alice Pattinson, who had "a small bindery near the British Museum".[28] Raised on *Hans Andersen's Tales* and the Bible, he favoured signed signed, limited vellum and yapp editions of Kipling, Maeterlinck, Ruskin, and illustrations by Beardsley, Edward Detmold, Rackham, Dulac, E. Garth Jones, Frank Brangwyn, Spencer Pryse, Granville Fell, Heath Robinson, Charles Robinson, Grasset and Willy Pogany.[29] His favourite binder was Cedric Chivers in Bath, who made at least dozen bindings for books Dunsany selected in shades of leafy greens and mauve, with front (and sometimes back) covers gold-tooled and inlaid with chivalric or faery scenes in opalescent colours.[30] Æ, whom Dunsany described as a "marvellous genius",[31] frequently used the word "opalescent"; "everything he saw was either opalescent or iridescent".[32] Dunsany's liking for opalescence led him to acquire, c. 1903, a fine silver cigar box set with a huge uncut opal, designed by Archibald Knox, and made by Liberty & Co.,[33] and a glistening gesso and mother-of-pearl portrait by Frank Pickford Marriott. Like his uncle Horace Plunkett, Dunsany also collected more restrained bindings by William Pender, a forwarder based in Edinburgh between c. 1905-1920, until he moved to Dublin c. 1921. An early example is a quarter binding for Walter Crane's illustrations to E. Spenser's *The Shepheard's Calendar*, stamped "1898" and "Pender Edin" on the inside cover, while the full green morocco binding of *The Booke of Thenseygnementes* (1904), blind-stamped with shamrocks in Dunsany's favourite green, was evidently made specially for him. Lord Dunsany also had Herrick's *Lyrical Poems* bound in "Old Rose Seal, Richly Tooled" and William Morris's *Life and Death of Jason* bound in "Crimson Crushed Levant, Tooled" by Pender.[34] Dramatic bindings of Dunsany's published writing included one in turquoise, gilded morocco for his admirer and fellow-charade player, E. Nesbit's quarterly, *The Neolith* (1907), where his work appeared beside that of Graily Hewitt, Spencer Pryse, Selwyn Image, and Edmund J. Sullivan; and his fifth book, *A Dreamer's Tales* (1910), illustrated by Sime, bound in "Scotch deerskin . . . specially tanned and dyed for Messrs Sangorski and Sutcliffe".[35] He also accumulated most of Sime's original illustrations for his books and had bought the six dramatically swirling pen and ink drawings by the major Celtic Revival illustrator, John Campbell (Seaghan MacCathmhaoil), for Mary A. Hutton's acclaimed translation of *The Táin* (1907), the heroic Ulster saga of the Fianna.[36]

Dunsany found himself being drawn into "what was known as the Irish renaissance", partly through his uncle but also on his own unfolding merits as a writer, while still nominally the (short-lived, if popular) Conservative candidate for West Wiltshire.[37] Yeats wrote to his father from Dunsany: "Dunsany is a man of genius I think . . . I want to get him into 'the movement' " and Dunsany wrote, "I have been among great men".[38] His commitment to writing tales "of spirits greater than man" led to his inclusion (with George Bernard Shaw and George Moore) in *The Shanachie* (1906-7), a landmark Irish literary miscellany with its striking cover design by Beatrice Elvery, an eminently versatile Arts and Crafts figure.[39] He also chaired the Dublin Arts Club meeting at which Yeats mourned the early death of John Millington Synge. His next book, *Time and the Gods* (1906), included a tale written around one of Sime's drawings, rather than the other (usual) way round. A trip to Paris to buy cast glass directly from Lalique, shortly after the birth of their son in 1906, inspired the first tale in what Æ thought his best book, *The Sword of Welleran* (1908),[40] written in snatched hours between intrepid travelling, residing in London, country house parties, playing cricket,[41] hunting, shooting, and stalking. He was encouraged by a "kind review" by the poet Edward Thomas and *The Saturday Review*'s open invitation to publish his writing, but he was gloomy about "the obscurity that seemed in those days to wrap" his "spiritual wanderings".[42] W.B. Yeats' invitation to write a play for the Abbey Theatre temporarily floored him until the poet taunted him that he would ask someone else to use Dunsany's idea; the result was *The Glittering Gate*, Dunsany's first of many plays, written in an afternoon and successfully performed in 1909.[43] Yeats and Lady Gregory became regular visitors to Dunsany, as did Æ, who found a jovial soulmate in Sime, "his conversation that of a scholar and a philosopher, his interests and knowledge vast and varied";[44] thus the poet Padraic Colum's wife thought Lord Dunsany "romantic and poetic-looking, and when he spoke at clubs and literary societies he was very persuasive, and he chanted poetry almost as beautifully as Yeats, and with immense excitement and enthusiasm, and he read his own plays to delighted audiences . . . Many people thought Lord Dunsany did not get the showing in the new movement commensurate with the importance of his work".[45]

Lord Dunsany's aversion to advertising, which included labels or any kind of documentation, makes the documentation of his collecting a challenge, particularly as he confirmed: "My concern was not with facts but with whatever fancy might rise up from my imagination after the beauty of what I saw had sunk into it".[46] Around this time, he started making clay seals, featuring mythical creatures like dragons and pegasi, even "a very fine effigy of my head", to adorn make-believe orders of merit for friends and young relations whose fanciful uniforms he also designed.[47] His love of the fantastic can be seen in three magnificent Pilkington's Royal Lancastrian ware lustre vases he purchased at the 1908 Franco-British Exhibition in London. On one, twenty inches tall, gilded Valkyrie ride on Walpurgis Night across a vibrant cobalt-blue ground, highlit with crimson;[48] on another, in the same colours, but with a vertical axis emphasised by falling flamelets, Orpheus plays the lyre to a wrapt group of wild animals (all-too-familiar targets to Dunsany), while on the other side Euridyce is consumed by hell fire, watched helplessly by Orpheus. Lightning flashes across the neck of the "Valkyrie" vase, formalised leaves decorate that of Orpheus. The Third, taller, more slender vase depicts "The Furies", Megaera, Tisiphone, and Alecto, described in gold lustre on Pilkington's "Fiery Crystalline" red glaze.[49] At the same exhibition, he also bought an eighteen-inch diameter lustre plaque of a gold and crimson galleon in full sail against a turquoise blue ground, designed by Gordon Forsyth and painted by Charles Cundall; the reverse is glazed in his beloved dark peacock green, painted with a large ornate carp and emblazoned with the monogram of Charles Cundall "PINX" and the 1908 year-mark of a cypress tree and signature dropping flamelets of Gordon Forsyth "DES". He also commissioned a further, smaller, exquisite lidded vase, which bears Gordon Forsyth's 1908 cypress tree year-mark and monogram;[50] it depicts an emblazoned galleon on stylised high seas painted in silver gilt lustre against his favourite dark forest green and is inscribed in large Roman capitals with lines from John Masefield, their friend and admired poet:

"THEY THAT GO DOWN TO THE SEA
IN SHIPS, THAT DO BUSINESS IN
GREAT WATERS; THESE SEE

THE WORKS OF THE LORD AND
HIS WONDERS
IN THE DEEP".

The lid bears the Dunsany crest of a horse, Pegasus, and antelope, motto "*Festina Lente*", and the neck a garland of Tudor roses. Abraham Lomax, chemist at the works between 1896-1911, presented a copy of his book (the first on the subject), *Royal Lancastrian Pottery* (1957), to Dunsany shortly before his death.

It is not recorded why the Dunsanys chose George Jack to design a new billiard room for Dunsany Castle in 1911. They had been seeing a lot of Yeats, whose name appears frequently in the Dunsany visitors' book, and who may well have been responsible for suggesting either the firm of his hero, William Morris or Jack himself. Yeats' sister, Lily, had worked as one of May Morris's embroidresses between 1888 and 1894, along with Mrs. George Jack and William De Morgan's sister Mary, while the Yeats family were living in Bedford Park. During this period, in 1890, George Jack assumed the role of chief furniture designer at Morris & Co. from Philip Webb, having "taken over Webb's architectural and design practice".[51] Dunsany also records partridge-shooting with Sir Hugh and Lady Bell around this time at Rounton Grange in Yorkshire, "a house built and decorated by the genius of William Morris and by the band of workers who were inspired by it".[52] He was introduced to the Bells through Sir Hugh's eminent Arabist daughter Gertrude, whom he had met in 1911, having read her desert travel book, *Amurath to Amurath*. In fact, Philip Webb had built the main house, while Jack designed a room there with arched top windows, like those in his Dunsany Billiard Room, executed some wood-carvings[53] and "did cottages and a village hall at East Rounton".[54]

George Jack (1855-1932), born of British parents on Long Island, had joined Philip Webb's office in the late 1870s, "principally to help with interior work. A skilful inlayer and carver, [he] became involved with furniture production at Morris & Co. when the workshop moved to Merton in 1881".[55] He taught carving at Central School of Arts and Crafts and at the Royal College of Art, both under W.R. Lethaby. When Jack made his first of four visits to Dunsany, in October 1911, he would have found that "little had been done to the castle" since James Shiel's alterations and additions of the 1840s in the Perpendicular gothic style, as "the one surviving scheme, produced by Gilbert Scott" for "what purported to be a new 'keep' " had been abandoned.[56] What Jack proposed was the current new "kind of organic approach" to "the country house as a country product rather than a seat of authority". In contrast to Scott's gravitas;[57] he emphasised "honest traditional building", what Webb called "the value of the Commonplace".[58] He paid homage to the old house with semi-vaulting, wood panelling, and compartmentalised plasterwork, while his delightfully modelled Webb and Gimson-inspired friezes inside and his external harling and slate roofing on small modular structures covering over what had been outdoor passages and inadequate servants' quarters recall Cotswold village buildings. His detailed "Cubing Book"[59] shows he did not only the Billiard Room, but a neighbouring roof, lavatory, WC, Gun Room, additional porch, Butler's pantry, men's room, and brushing room. The exterior gable end of the Billiard Room bears an inscribed date, "1912", although his subsequent repairs to the roof and main castle walls were not concluded until 1914. The focus in the room was the intricately carved oak fireplace, executed by J. Milligan and Jack, who carved the coat of arms and two side panels;[60] it was set in green Connemara marble and adorned, like the walls, with amorial shields of families related to the Dunsanys;[61] the nineteen shields were painted by E.W. Tristram, the English mediaevalist art historian, who also taught at the Royal College of Art, and belonged to the Walpole Society along with E.S. Prior and W.R. Lethaby. The builders, the long-established Belfast contractors, McLaughlin & Harvey, who had opened a Dublin office in 1899, and a London branch in 1905, worked with all the most progressive Irish architects of the time.[62]

Dunsany liked "to see a century looking like a century, and not ashamed of itself, aping some better century". He thought "the essential thing about design is not whether Jacobean, Queen Anne or Georgian is the correcter period, but whether the design is alive or dead, whether the craftsman is trying to make something beautiful or something correct". In true Arts and Crafts mode, he wrote, "There is a joy, or at least a contentment, in trying to do beautiful work, and this joy or contentment will shine back out of the work, to illuminate the spirits of others and become part of pleasant memories . . . and it will be the intention of the worker to give this pleasure, and he will be glad to think he has done it."[63] He detested sham, imitators, or so-called antiques. What he wanted was "live work" and true craftsmanship, which coincided with the ideals expressed by Jack in an article, "From an Architect's Point of View" which he wrote as part of a series on "Modern British Plasterwork" in *The Architectural Review*. "Just enough and no more" should be the motto of all plaster artists, he wrote, heartily advocating cooperation between the architect and craftsman, while he and Ernest Gimson agreed "the plasterer should go to Nature for his ideas" and be skilled at modelling. The amount of relief, the question of natural light, the "subtlety and beauty of plaster" worked wet *in situ*, and the application of ornament to the ceiling were other crucial issues.[64] His plasterwork at Dunsany features oak and shamrock leaves compartmentalised with rectilinear interlaced sections on the ceiling, while the upper wall friezes depict in deeper relief hares, rabbits, squirrels, snipe, pheasants, partridges, hedgehogs and other game birds among wild flowers, dog roses, oak, holly, iris, sorbus, ferns, and other leaves. A white linen damask table-cloth echoes these creatures amongst foliage.

The new room was furnished with carpets that had caught Dunsany's eye in North and East Africa and the Near East, and with the pelts and heads of the many animals he hunted and shot: "We can throw a few hyena skins down by the fireplace in the billiard room".[65] Around its walls, Dunsany arranged carefully chosen pieces of furniture by the man he called "our great craftsman", Ernest Gimson, "an honest craftsman" who "must have found it harder to get employment than any crafts-man had ever found it before" in the face of the "thriving genuine-antique-mongers".[66] In August 1916, Gimson made a drawing for the elegant, bevelled glass showcase in English walnut, inlaid with holly and ebony, that Dunsany had com-missioned. It is not recorded what was originally shown in the showcase, perhaps drawings, the imaginary insignia he mod-elled, or his own calligraphic flourishes, exquisitely bound. Gimson had already supplied Dunsany with a chest lavishly inlaid with a dog rose design, set with his signature Japonist "Samurai helmet" silver lock plate and mounted on a simple (holly?) stand,[67] and a small writing table with a drawer and delightful stretcher. John Cornforth records that the chest, which he describes as "a cabinet", was "one of a group of pieces acquired at the Paris [Arts Decoratifs de Grande-Bretagne et d'Irlande] exhibition of 1914", although it is not specifically listed in the catalogue.[68] Mary Greensted considers a large, wooden handled, chamfered oak writing desk with a hayrake stretcher, derived from vernacular wood-working tra-dition,[69] and a couple of latticework chairs may be by Peter Waals, and date from the 1920s.[70]

Lord Dunsany acquired at least two further Arts and Crafts pieces for this room by major Cotswold figures, who answered his conception of art as adding "something to the world that was not there already".[71] Both date from the mid-1920s. One is a large, deep, Wedgwood earthenware platter, painted in black, silver, and gold with the Dunsany family coat of arms by Louise Powell, with her husband Alfred, colleagues of Gimson at Sapperton. The Dunsany motto, "*Festina Lente*", is painted in gold on a scroll, set against a flowery meadow, while the rim is painted with alternating sprigs of green oak leaves and brown acorns. On the back, it is numbered '2562', signed with Louise Powell's monogram, and dated "Nov. 1925". Mary Greensted writes that,

> "by 1930 [Powell] was being acclaimed as one of the finest living brushwork artists. Many of the items [she and her husband] produced were for special commissions such as the decorative platters over twenty inches in diameter, affectionately called 'Mrs Powell's bread and butters'. These were designed for displaying along a frieze above wall panellings in English country houses. Sometimes they were painted with views of the house itself or the owner's coat-of-arms."[72]

The potter Gordon Forsyth thought the Powells "excellent artists", even if they were not actually making the Wedgwood pottery they decorated: "Their best work is found in lordly bowls and plaques . . . based on the brave and honest pattern work of William Morris . . . English pottery would be very much poorer without their splendid contributions to the artistic side of the craft."[73]

The other piece is a superb mahogany print cabinet designed by Gordon Russell in 1923, and made by Edgar Turner and H. Linton for the Russell Workshops in

Broadway at Linton's premises in Pitfield Street, Hoxton. It was described by Russell as being "veneered with quartered Walnut, finely figured and with borders of Laburnum oysterwood and Ebony lines" on a "stand of ebony", 3' 8" x 2' 2" x 5' 1" high, "the legs being chamfered and shaped", with ornate hinges and "handles of polished Bronze pierced and backed with Blue Velvet"[74] by the metal craftsman S.H. Gardiner. The cabinet shows Russell synthesising the earlier influences of Gimson and the Barnsleys with that of seventeenth century furniture in a daring, virtuoso piece. Russell, whose manifesto for modern design, *Honesty and the Crafts* was published the same year, later wrote:

"We were beginning to produce cabinet-work of high quality and our status as furniture makers was confirmed by an invitation to send some exhibits to the Palace of Arts at the British Empire Exhibition at Wembley the next year, 1924. Our principal exhibit there, a walnut cabinet on an ebony base, was made by Edgar Turner whilst he was at Shoreditch. Lord Dunsany bought it at the exhibition for £200 and in doing so gave us most powerful help at a critical juncture—not that we made any profit out of it, for we cut up half a ton of ebony to make the base, but his gesture proved that there were people who would pay prices for good modern work which compared with those paid for antiques. This greatly impressed my family, in addition to getting us a good deal of useful publicity outside. My ambition was to produce furniture of the highest possible standard of workmanship in which the best material would speak for itself, so that in my designs I tried to make the most of these qualities".[75]

Dunsany had earlier commissioned a fine set of Irish Arts and Crafts furniture in subtly carved oak, decorated in Celtic Revival zoomorphic interlace, for a bedroom above the new billiard room. This was made by the Bray Art Furniture Industry in County Wicklow, whose founder, manager, designer, and instructor in cabinet-making and carving, Sophia St. John Whitty, shared his Ruskinian admiration of truth to nature in craftsmanship and Horace Plunkett's dedication to "The Development of National Art", the title of an essay she wrote.[76] When she was not in the workshop pursuing her ideal "of an unselfish love of beauty and conscientious workmanship" along the lines of a Florentine craft guild, she would gather village children around her studio fire "to hear Irish fairy tales and folklore".[77] In 1910, she became a member of Sir Horace Plunkett's United Irishwomen with their commitment to women's home industries, but continued to direct a thriving class, industry, and retail shop until the outbreak of War. As usual, any labels on the Dunsany furniture have disappeared. The Celtic interlace theme in this room was continued in a colour-stained pokerwork frame, inscribed with the arms of the Four Provinces of Ireland, made by the Belfast-based group of craftswomen known as the Irish Decorative Art Association. It framed one of a series of haunting watercolours of a misty Connemara heather and mountain bog landscapes painted between 1904-1912 by the Irish artist and songwriter, Percy French.[78]

There remains one further legacy of Lord Dunsany's involvement with the Irish Arts and Crafts movement: the limited edition of two hundred and fifty copies of *Selections from the Writings of Lord Dunsany*, hand-printed and published by Elizabeth Corbet Yeats at her Cuala Press in Churchtown, Dundrum "in the County of Dublin". Her signature colophon records that the volume was "finished on Lady Day, in the Year Nineteen Hundred and Twelve". In his introduction,

W.B. Yeats describes how he tried to persuade Dunsany to leave "those magic lands of his with their vague Eastern air" for "the old Irish legendary world", but realised he "could not, without losing his rich beauty of careless suggestion". Numbering Dunsany among the stars of the Irish literary revival, he muses over how in his writing he has "transfigured with beauty the common sights of the world", his travellers recalling the "fabulous beauty" of "imagined colours, ceremonies and incredible processions" imbued with "the pathos of fragility". For Yeats, his plays and stories evoke "some old Irish jewel work", "a sword covered with Indian Arabesques", or "cloud palaces at the sundown". This evocative sense of bemused enchantment, coupled with the qualities of human endeavour and skill advocated by Lethaby[79] and eminently sustained by Elizabeth Yeats's Cuala Press,[80] may be seen not only in Dunsany's writings but also in the unexpected range of treasures he collected.

Acknowledgments

To Alan Crawford, without whose initial encouragement this article might not have been written, and for his continuing help. Also to the 20th Baron Dunsany, Patrick Bowe, Mary Greensted, Amy Clarke, Trevor Chinn and Ray Leigh, Ann Martha Rowan, Colum O'Riordan, Edward Murphy, Pete James, Anthony Hobbs, Caroline Walsh, and John Searle.

Endnotes

[1] Dunsany, *Patches of Sunlight* (London: William Heinemann, 1938), p. 23.

[2] His melancholic mother was a cousin of Sir Richard Burton (1821-90), explorer, scholar, soldier, anthropologist, linguist,

writer, and translator, affamed for his translations of *The Arabian Nights* (1885-8).

[3] The oldest parts of Dunsany Castle, "a pair of tower blocks, each with two towers . . . obviously the original keep", bear witness to its original role as a defence of the Pale in the late twelfth century. There were Plunketts settled in County Meath by the early fourteenth century and there have been Barons Dunsany by writ since 1439 and by letter since 1462. Their unbroken residence at Dunsany is miraculous given the vicissitudes of Irish history and the waxing and waning of their fortunes and lands. See John Cornforth, "Dunsany Castle, Co. Meath—I, The Seat of Lord Dunsany" in *Country Life*, 17 May 1971, pp. 1296-1399.

[4] Dunsany, *The Curse of the Wise Woman* (London: William Heinemann, 1933), although in this occasionally autobiographical novel the house is meant to be imaginary; quoted in Mark Amory, *Lord Dunsany, A Biography* (London: Collins, 1972), p.18.

[5] Dunsany, 1938, p. 67. His first poem was published in the *Pall Mall Magazine* in 1896.

[6] Dunsany, 1938, p. 5.

[7] Simon Heneage and Henry Ford, *Sidney Sime, Master of the Mysterious* (London: Thames and Hudson, 1980), pp. 25-6. This tale remained unfinished.

[8] Amory records a friend of his saying, "He looks as if he'd stood naked and had his clothes hurled at him, leaving them wherever they happened to land. In the country, where he bicycled long distances, he wore "rabbity clothes", retorting

"Why spoil good ones?" (Amory, 1972, p. 32).

[9] For example: "As I walked through the countryside at the end of June the roving spirit remained with me and I walked right across Ireland", "I walked by myriads of fox-gloves and briar-roses, past bogs and hills and lakes", wrapt by the beauties of nature; then, "I rowed the whole length of the Blackwater" (Dunsany, 1938, p. 261).

[10] Letter from the Rt. Hon. Horace Plunkett to Lady Betty Balfour, July 1899, quoted in *Seventy Years Young. Memories of Elizabeth, Countess of Fingall*, told to Pamela Hinkson (London: Collins, 1937), p. 251. He continued, "I shall try to get him to do a little literary work". Plunkett, who was knighted in 1903, was committed to a programme of stimulating Ireland's material prosperity by apolitical means. In 1899, his careful steering of the Liberal Government's programme of de-anglicisation resulted in the introduction of the Department of Agriculture and Technical Instruction, the guiding body behind the Arts and Crafts movement in Ireland.

[11] Letter from Plunkett to Lady Betty Balfour, 1897, quoted in Margaret Digby, *Horace Plunkett, An Anglo-American Irishman* (Oxford: Basil Blackwell, 1949), p. 152. Lines by his eighteen-year old nephew were about to appear in *The Irish Homestead*.

[12] Horace Plunkett in *The Gael* (New York), March 1902, p. 81.

[13] See Nicola Gordon Bowe and Elizabeth S. Cumming, *The Arts and Crafts Movements in Dublin and Edinburgh* (Dublin: Irish Academy Press 1998), pp. 184-8 et al. In 1905, Æ became the outstanding editor of *The Irish Homestead*. Sydney Brooks would write in 1912 of Sir Horace Plunkett's Department of Agriculture and Technical Instruction that "it became under

his guidance the one radiating centre . . . of sound economic thought and practice" in Ireland, "rehabilitating rural life as a social organism" and encouraging women to "bring into Ireland the desire for beauty and comfort which are the beginnings of civilization". ("Sir Horace Plunkett and his Work", *Fortnightly Review*, Vol. 97, June 1912, p. 1020.

[14] Trevor West, *Horace Plunkett, Co-operation and Politics: An Irish Biography*, Gerards Cross: Colin Smyth, 1986, p. 88. Plunkett, who loved the theatre, numbered all the most progressive Irish poets, playwrights and writers from all walks of life among his acquaintance, entertaining them, using the newspapers he bought up to publicise their "passionate conviction . . . that if Irish traditions, literature, language, art, music, and culture are allowed to disappear, it will mean the disappearance of the race". Horace Plunkett, *Irish in the New Century* (London: John Murray, 1905), p. 150.

[15] The supplement was loosely influenced by Patrick Geddes's "Northern Seasonal", *The Evergreen*, published in Edinburgh between 1896-7.

[16] West, 1986, p. 5.

[17] Dunsany, 1938, p. 111. He was continually discouraged by relations "who obviously rated my writing as far interior to any serious work, such as fattening cattle".

[18] *Ibid.*

[19] See Lord Dunsany, "Sime", *The Fortnightly Review* (August 1942), and the Bibliography in Heneage and Ford, 1980, pp. 32-4.

[20] Dunsany, 1938, p. 155. When Dunsany showed Sime "a story and asked him if it accurately described what was going on in the picture he said: 'It sounds extremely probable' ".

[21] Fingall, 1937, p. 314. Tragically, the house was razed during the 1922 Irish Civil War.

[22] Trevor West, *Horace Plunkett, Co-operation and Politics: An Irish Biography* (Gerrards Cross: Colin Smythe, 1986), p. 87.

[23] Amory, 1972, p. 34.

[24] Dunsany, 1938, p. 80.

[25] "The Haunting of Whitebeams" is a story in his octavo volume *The Last Revolution* (1919), p. 390, where his coloured pencil and pen and ink text is overwritten on top of the initial pencil hand of his wife.

[26] Particularly beautiful is *The Last of the Unicorns*, an octavo volume bound in white vellum, gilded and stained with a green-plumed peacock. Prefaced by a newspaper cutting, "It is an awful responsibility to have been allowed to survive the great war", its first page is dated 25 April 1919.

[27] See account of the first exhibition of works by Cockerell's students of the Central School of Arts and Crafts, London in *The Studio*, Vol. XV, 1899, p. 46. See also Esther Wood, "British Tooled Bookbindings and their Designers" in Modern Bookbindings and their Designers, *The Studio*, Special Winter Number, London 1899-1900, pp. 38-47.

[28] See Mary Greensted and Sophia Wilson (eds.), *Originality and Initiative: The Arts and Crafts Archives at Cheltenham*

(Cheltenham, 2003), p.114 and fig. 76. Cockerell's binding for Emery Walker of 1902, fig. 68, bears a strong resemblance to a blank volume acquired by Dunsany around this time.

[29] Perhaps because of his acquaintance with T.W. Rolleston, a critical archivist in the Arts and Crafts Society of Ireland and manager of the Irish Industries Association, he acquired a special purple suede bound copy of Rolleston's retelling of Wagner's *Parsifal* (London 1913) with Pogany's illustrations (See Bowe and Cumming, 1998, 180-1).

[30] Chivers (c.1853-1929) developed a method of hand over-sewing, in which the stitches pass diagonally through the paper, thus helping to eliminate strain due to side pull, but it was the decorative "Vellucent" bindings he developed c. 1903 that appealed to Dunsany. The technique was designed "to protect covers bearing coloured designs (usually pictorial in nature) painted on paper, attached to the boards, and then covered with transparent vellum". It lent itself to "highly decorative designs" as "mother-of-pearl, iridescent shell, and the like" could be "covered and permanently protected by the vellum", whose surface could be further enhanced by gold tooling.
(http://palimpsest.stanford.edu/don/dt/dt3692.html),
3 December 2004. I am indebted to Elizabeth S. Cumming for her information on Chivers.

[31] Letter from Lord Dunsany to his wife, 21 March 1908, quoted in Amory, 1972, p. 60.

[32] "It is apparently the colour of all visitants from the spiritual world, and in order to show off, they always take care, according to Russell, to have a background of purple and violet cloud . . . before . . . they . . . rise and waver into irides-

cent vapour": The Revd. Stopford Brooke, letter, 6 June 1898, quoted in C.H. Rolleston, *Portrait of an Irishman: A Biographical Sketch of T.W. Rolleston* (London: Methuen, 1939), p. 26.

[33] For a similar design, see A.J. Tilbrooke, *The Designs of Archibald Knox for Liberty & Co.*, Sheperton Beauchamp, 1955. Knox had visited Dublin in the early 1890s to study Celtic treasures. See Anthony Jones, *Knox of Man and Liberty of London*; and Isabelle Anscombe, *A Sense of Place: Knox, Manx Nationalism and the Celtic Revival* (2001). In Stephen A. Martin (ed.), *Archibald Knox* (London: Artmedia). Dunsany also seems to have collected work by Edward Spencer's Artificers' Guild.

[34] Catalogue of Sixth Exhibition of The Arts and Crafts Society of Ireland (Dublin 1921), nos. 117 and 118. Pender subsequently bound and tooled the iconic eight-volume sets, printed on handmade paper in a limited edition of 100 copies by Maunsel & Roberts of *Ireland's Memorial Records 1914-1918*, illustrated by Harry Clarke (1923). He is remembered, along with Sir Edward Sullivan Bt. and Eleanor Kelly, as one of the three principal binders of the Irish Arts and Crafts movement. See Colm O Lochlainn, "Book-binding in Ireland" in F.R. Higgins (ed.), *Progress in Irish Printing* (Dublin: A. Thom and Co., 1936), p. 107. I am grateful to Elizabeth S. Cumming for tracing Pender's Edinburgh whereabouts. See Bowe and Cummings (1998), pp. 105 and 126.

[35] Of which it was noted inside the covers: "Deerskin is a good-looking and durable leather which has rarely been used for bookbinding purposes since the Middle Ages. It has been prepared free from injurious acids and the natural grain preserved. The deer were killed owing to shortage of food during the Great War".

[36] See R.A. Dawson, "An illustrator of Celtic romance", *The Studio*, October 1909. Both John Campbell and his brother Joseph exhibited with the Arts and Crafts Society of Ireland.

[37] Thus, "while my fancy travelled these lands [of the imagination] in the early evening, I was explaining Tariff Reform to some village each day at eight o'clock"; and "We had several more shooting visits and some fox-hunting and I wrote three more tales"; "on January 17th I went up to the attic after tea and wrote 'A Night at the Inn' in one sitting". (Dunsany, 1938, pp. 145 and 180-1).

[38] Amory, 1972, p. 63. The Dunsanys' initial rapture over Yeats cooled when the poet seemed to become increasingly jealous of Dunsany, perhaps for his richly aristocratic blood, his seemingly throwaway, utterly uncontrived access to an imaginary world of his own making which attracted increasing success, and for his effortless sportsmanship—a true courtier in the Renaissance image Yeats invoked. Yeats' own beliefs in the spirit world were well-known from his seminal book, *The Celtic Twilight* (1893 and 1902).

[39] See Bowe and Cumming, 1998, pp. 126-32 *et al.*

[40] Æ wrote of his "great admiration" for Dunsany's stories: "He strides on the master-ship{?} of the world of phantasy amazingly. There are large splashes of genius in him, I think", quoted in Clifford Bax, *Rosemary for Remembrance* (London: Frederick Muller, 1948), p. 60. In 1908, Dunsany offered Æ money to start up a paper to give Irish poets a voice.

[41] Dunsany had his own cricket ground at Dunsany Castle. Mark Bence-Jones writes that "the chief Ascendancy game

was, of course, cricket ... Among the patrons of Irish cricket [were] Lord Dunsany" who in 1906 became a member of Na Shuler, the exclusive club which was the Irish equivalent of I Zingari.

[42] Dunsany 1938, pp. 142-3.

43 He wrote another play that year in the evening between the hours of six and nine. "I was due at a party at nine-thirty and just got the play done in time" (Dunsany, 1938, p. 159).

[44] Letter from Lady Dunsany, 20 October 1910, quoted in Amory, 1972, p.73.

[45] Mary Colum, *Life and the Dream* (London: Macmillan, 1947), pp. 108-9.

[46] Dunsany, 1938, p. 139.

[47] Dunsany, 1938, p. 188. The most picturesque was for his wife's sister's daughter, Lady Pansy Pakenham (subsequently married to the Bloomsbury painter Henry Lamb) and her Pansyovsky Regiment of Pansieland. Stars modelled from gold or silver sealing wax accompanied the beribboned medals.

[48] The Shapes of both these blue vases are identified with a "2471" impression on their bases. See Anthony J. Cross, *Pilkington's Royal Lancastrian Pottery and Tiles* (London, 1980), p. 75. Cross writes: "Two versions of the Valkyrie vase exist; one owned by Lord Dunsany, the other by Manchester City Art Gallery. The latter differs in several respects from that owned by Lord Dunsany but it is apparent that the design is taken from a water-colour by Gordon Forsyth illustrated in colour in the Studio Year Book for 1909" (p. 44). Forsyth's "contribution to

the company's success" as chief artist at Pilkington's between 1905 and 1916 cannot, Cross states, "be overstressed" (p. 59).

[49] All three are impressed on the base with the factory's year-mark for 1906-12; the "Valkyrie" and "Furies" bear Gordon Forsyth's distinctive 1908 year-mark of a cypress, clumps of grass, and wavy lines, while the "Orpheus" is marked "VI", indicating the year of its manufacture, 1906.

[50] I am grateful to Mr. Cross for his confirmation that the green ship vase with inscription was included in Pilkington's Franco-British exhibition.

[51] Charles Harvey and Jon Press, *William Morris. Design and Enterprise in Victorian Britain* (Manchester: Manchester University Press, 1991), p. 177. A wooden chest by George Jack was singled out in the official Irish report of the English Loan Collection at the first exhibition of the Arts and Crafts Society of Ireland in 1895 as an excellent example of work by a designer who was able to skilfully execute his own designs.

[52] Dunsany 1938, p. 198. Routon Grange is now demolished. The Jack Archive (at the William Morris Gallery, Walthamstow) includes a photograph of a plasterwork frieze at Dunsany with a reference to a "very similar frieze" in the dining room at a house designed by Mervyn Macartney at Minster, Munstead, Sussex. Although illustrated in the *Architectural Review* (March 1908, Vol. XXIII, no. 136, pp. 224-5), there is no evidence (as yet) to suggest Dunsany saw this frieze, which is almost identical to that at Dunsany. It would doubtless have appealed to him with its nesting pheasants, squirrels, hedgehogs, and hares amidst rose hips, ferns, oak leaves and acanthus, beneath an arabesque of compartmentalised leaves; the Dunsany fire-place, elaborately carved by Jack, differs, however, from the

plain one in Sussex, which is dominated by two large owls. The photograph of the Dunsany plasterwork frieze was taken by Thomas Lewis, the Birmingham architectural photographer, who visited Dunsany in 1913, where he took at least four (hitherto untraced) photographs. I am indebted to Alan Crawford and Pete James of the Birmingham Central Library for this information.

[53] According to Amy Clarke, whose research appears in this issue of the DAS Journal.

[54] "Between 1902 and 1907 Jack was in practice with T. Hamilton Crawford, while continuing and completing Philip Webb's work", A. Stuart Gray, *Edwardian Architecture: A Biographical Dictionary* (London 1985), p. 219. Jack's book, *Woodwork, Design and Workmanship* (1903) was published in Lethaby's Artistic Crafts Series of Technical Handbooks.

[55] Jeremy Cooper, *Victorian and Edwardian Décor* (New York, 1987), p. 165.

[56] John Cornforth, "Dunsany Castle, Co. Meath—II, The Seat of Lord Dunsany", *Country Life*, 3 June 1971, pp. 1365-6. Gavin Stamp writes: "Sir Gilbert Scott was invited to enlarge Dunsany Castle, a Mediaeval structure extensively Gothicised in the late 18th and early 19th centuries, and apparently designed the new stables and, possibly, a lodge. George Gilbert Scott junior surveyed the building in 1872", but that the proposed additions were "partly abandoned", *An Architect of Promise. George Gilbert Scott junior (1839-1897) and the Late Gothic Revival* (Donington: Shaun Tyas, 2002), p. 376. I am grateful to Gavin Stamp for drawing my attention to this.

[57] Mark Girouard, *Life in the English Country House: A Social and Architectural History* (New Haven: Yale University Press, 1989), p. 306). Girouard stresses the increased informality in all aspects of life and the care given to the restoration of old houses during this period.

[58] Mark Girouard, *Sweetness and Light: The Queen Anne Movement 1860-1900* (New Haven: Yale University Press, 1977), p. 120; see W.R. Lethaby, *Philip Webb and his Work* (Oxford: Oxford University Press, 1935).

[59] Housed in the Jack collection, William Morris Gallery, Walthamstow. I am grateful to Alan Crawford for drawing my attention to this, and to Amy Clarke for photocopying the relevant pages.

[60] This was exhibited as "Fireplace in New Room at Dunsany Castle, Ireland" at the 10th Arts and Crafts Exhibition Society in London in 1912, catalogue no. 71, where it is recorded as having been executed by McLoughlin and Harvey, the established Irish building contractors, assisted by Henry Elliot, foreman. The *Westminster Gazette* liked the "excellent treatment of grey and green marble", but not the overmantel (document J1129[a], Jack collection, William Morris Gallery). I am grateful to Amy Clarke for sending me a copy of this and to Alan Crawford for transcribing it.

[61] Dunsany's mother had assumed by Royal Licence on 20 December 1905 the surnames of Ernle and Drax, and the arms of Drax, Erle, and Ernle.

[62] In 1912, they were carrying out domestic work for Major Stern, Dunsany's neighbour, at Bective House, Co. Meath, for the Queen Anne Revival architects McDonnell and Reid.

[63] Dunsany, *While the Sirens Slept* (London: Jarrolds, 1944), p. 99. I am indebted to Patrick Bowe for discovering this reference.

[64] Laurence Turner, George Jack, Ernest Gimson and Walter Gilbert respectively on "Modern British Plasterwork—I, II and III", *The Architectural Review*, March-June 1908, pp. 220-278.

[65] Letter to Lady Dunsany from the Sahara, 7 December 1913, quoted Amory, 1972, p. 99.

[66] Dunsany, 1944, p. 100.

[67] I am most indebted to Mary Greensted, who dates this to c. 1905-15, and gives the undated design for the inlay as no. 1941.223.339 in the Cheltenham Art Gallery and Museum's Gimson archive. There is also a related entry in the one surviving workshop book for 1916.

[68] Cornforth, 3 June 1971, p.1367. The exhibition, which took place at the Pavillon de Marsan in the Louvre between April and October 1914, had a large English Arts and Crafts furniture section; it included a number of elaborate pieces designed by Jack and by Gimson, as well as a "*commode en noyer marquete, sur piedestal*" executed by P. Van der Waals (no. 1193).

[69] See Greensted, 1980, p. 119.

[70] Letter, 18 March 2004. The Dutch cabinetmaker Waals had gone to work as foreman, in close co-operation with Gimson, at the Daneway House workshops in Sapperton in 1902.

[71] Dunsany, 1938, p. 235.

[72] Anon., "Pottery Design and Decoration" in *Good Workmanship with Happy Thought: the work of Alfred and Louise Powell*, an exhibition organised by Cheltenham Art Gallery and Museums (1992), p. 19. Greensted writes (3.10.03) that the Powell archives are scant and "there are no surviving workshop books".

[73] His report on the Ceramic Section of the 1925 Paris International Exhibition quoted in Mary Greensted, *The Arts and Crafts Movement in the Cotswolds* (Stroud: Alan Sutton, 1996), p. 106.

[74] Gordon Russell's own description, handwritten on the back of one of the original photographs of the piece, is recorded as Design No. 61, photographed by G. Roper and Dennis Moss of Cirencester, 1923 (transcribed by permission of the Gordon Russell Trust Archive). The Trust still has the original drawings.

[75] Gordon Russell, *Designer's Trade: An Autobiography* (London, 1968), p. 125. I am grateful to Ray Leigh and Trevor Chinn of the Gordon Russell Trust for sending me information from the Trust's Archive; here, the price of the cabinet is given as £225.0.0., and Russell's handwriting on the back of its original photograph records "it was sold to Lord Dunsany within ten days of the opening of the exhibition".

[76] In the fourth issue of the *Journal and Proceedings of the Arts and Crafts Society of Ireland* (Dublin, 1906). See Bowe and Cumming, 1998, pp. 199-202.

[77] Her memoirs were published posthumously as *The Flaming Wheel: Nature Studies in the Counties of Dublin and Wicklow* (Dublin, 1924), where she recorded that, "No inferior mate-

rial was to be used, or imperfect work allowed where it would be out of sight". See Bowe and Cumming, 1998, pp. 199-202.

[78] French, from a landed family in County Roscommon, had worked as a civil engineer with the architect, Richard Caulfield Orpen until c. 1892, when he turned to the stage, popular songs and paintings, while Orpen became a major figure in the formative years of the Arts and Crafts Society of Ireland (whose catalogue title page he designed in 1895).

[79] Gifford Lewis writes of the Press that "it was the only offshoot from the Doves Press to survive in the original ideal form as handcraft, producing books as Lethaby had wanted, 'made by a human being for a human being' ", *The Yeats Sisters and the Cuala* (Dublin, 1994), p. 181. See also Liam Miller, *The Dun Emer Press, later the Cuala Press* (Dublin, 1973). See Bowe and Cumming 1998, pp. 205-8.

[80] Elizabeth Years was encouraged by Emery Walker, whom she had met in Bedford Park as early as 1888, through her family's friendship with William Morris and his circle, to study printing; when she and her brother were setting up the Dun Emer (subsequently Cuala) Press, he advised her to adopt 14-point Caslon Old Style as a readable, clear typeface, an untrimmed, rag, mould-made paper, "firm, crisp and thin", light ivory in tone, and a small quarto size similar to that of the Doves Press he had co-founded two years earlier, in 1900, with Cobden-Sanderson. See Bowe and Cumming, 1998, pp. 205-10.

Reviews

The Wanderer in Unknown Realms
by John Connolly; illustrated by Emily Hall
Bad Dog Books, July 2013, 114 pages

Although he is best known as a mystery writer, John Connolly's interest in the macabre was apparent as early as his first novel, *Every Dead Thing* (1999), which introduced his homicide detective-turned-private eye Charlie Parker. As readers of this series know, there is something rather uncanny about Mr. Parker and the cases in which he finds himself involved. In these stories Mr. Connolly reminds us that *mystery* has more than one meaning, and that the more mundane meaning is by no means the most appropriate one to apply in this instance.

In addition to the Parker mysteries, Mr. Connolly has also written *Nocturnes*, a collection of ghostly tales. These tales are firmly in the tradition of M.R. James and J.S. Le Fanu, which is to say that they present a more or less conventional view of the supernatural, featuring spirits of the damned and the daemonic entities that torment them, in accordance with the rules of folklore and the tenets of Christianity, in its Catholic guise. In this latest work, though, Mr. Connolly tentatively embraces the modern weird of Algernon Blackwood and William Hope Hodgson, and especially of the American author H. P. Lovecraft, who the late science fiction grandmaster Fritz Leiber called the "Copernicus of the horror story [who] shifted the focus of supernatural dread from man and his little world and his gods, to the stars and the black unplumbed gulfs of intergalactic space."

The story begins with our protagonist, a former British officer and survivor of the Somme who is called Mr. Soter, being summoned by a rather formidable solicitor, Mr. Quayle, to investigate the disappearance, about one week earlier, of one of their clients, Mr. Maulding, on behalf of the latter's nephew, who stands to inherit in the event that anything ill has befallen his uncle. Mr. Maulding "is among the most private of men, and begrudges any time spent away from his home." When Mr. Soter arrives at that home, we begin to understand: Mr. Maulding, who survived polio as a child and endured much loneliness as a result, has fash-ioned for himself a fortress of solitude where he may be alone with his one great love: books. Mr. Soter is amazed at the size and variety of Maulding's collection: "Even the reading rooms of the British Library itself seemed to pale beside it." The British Library is of course one of the prime repositories of human knowledge, and this implies that Mr. Maulding has surpassed it in an effort that Faustus might have envied. Among the books in the bedroom of the miss-ing recluse are several volumes of occult philosophy, and yet while the collection as a whole is almost compulsively organised, Soter can find no other books on this subject. In examining Maulding's correspondence, he discovers that he has been purchasing large quantities of books related to this area of study, and that most of them were purchased from two firms, one known to him and the other not known. When it develops that Maulding had made several previously unknown trips to London to purchase books, he follows the trail and finds himself immersed in the equally twilight worlds of occult secret societies and book scouts who can, for the right fee, locate any book, regardless of rarity. As Soter discovers, Mr. Maulding had set his sight on the rarest of the rare, a book compared to which *Al Azif* and the *Nine Gates to the Kingdom of Darkness* are as common as used J. K. Rowlings paperbacks: *Terrae Incognita*. Unknown Lands.

The idea of forbidden knowledge that might transform the world is a familiar one in weird fiction, but it is the suggestion that the wounded post-war world might have created the conditions favourable for this transformation that enriches Connolly's narrative with a meaning beyond its mere plot. Many of the characters are touched by losses from the war, and it is suggested that the war itself provided the circumstances for the world to be changed: "Evil calls to evil, and the circumstances are right . . . The fabric of existence was torn: the world was made ready for the book, and the book was ready for the world." The idea of a book that can overwrite all of existence is familiar to use from John Carpenter's film *In the Mouth of Madness* and Fred Chappell's story "The Adder", and there are element reminiscent of Stephen King's "The Mist", but while these works deal with the corruption of the world, Connolly implies, or rather comes out and states plainly, that it was the seeds of evil planted in the old world that bore fruit in the war, and that this fruit is what sustains the ultimate doom that befalls the world of Connolly's creations.

One of the hallmarks of the detective story is that it deals with both the introduction of chaos into a miniature of the world, as well as its resolution. This has never fully been the situation in the Charlie Parker novels (Parker survives, but barely, and usually with unbearable consequences compared to which death seems a mercy), and Mr. Soter, having stared into the abyss, finds himself under unwelcome scrutiny. He is a wounded paladin lost in a wasteland as bleak as Mr. Eliot's; he is the wanderer in unknown realms, and he knows what rough beast, its hour come round at last, slouches towards Bethlehem to be born.

Many of Mr. Connolly's stories have not, in my estimation, measured up to the promise of his novels, but he has shown, with *The Wanderer in Unknown Realms*, that this may simply be due to his need for a larger canvas to encompass his vision in all its ontological and eschatological sublimity.

Scott Connors

℘

Aleister Crowley: Wandering the Waste
by Martin Hayes, with art by R.H. Stewart
Markosia, May 2013, 144 pages

"Do what thou wilt shall be the whole of the Law."

Irish graphic novelist Martin Hayes's *Aleister Crowley: Wandering the Waste*, through its ambiguity in relation to the narratorial voice (an elderly Crowley), and through its use of multiple perspectives (news articles and other intertextual devices), operates to undermine the credibility of its characters, actions, and situations. Hayes's use of Crowley's reminiscences as the story's primary narrative serves to highlight the subjective, provisional nature of the biography, the role of the storyteller therein and, thus, calls into question historical accuracy—and even its very importance.

On the level of narrative technique, this position is reflected by the fact that the reader is often presented with a certain interpretation that is later undermined. To a certain degree, any biography of Crowley would be metafiction, as Hayes points out:

> "With Crowley it's all but impossible. He certainly wasn't averse to playing with the truth in order to

bathe himself in a more rarefied light. So many of the stories have two or three different versions, none of which may actually be the truth."

Another metafictional attribute of Hayes's graphic novel is its insistence on history as a form of discourse. Extending the metafictional critique of the realist narrative, Hayes's narrative asserts not only that the historical narrative is dependent upon signifiers masquerading as reality, but that history itself is a construct of conventions of narrative, language and ideology specifically ordered to generate the illusion of objective representation.

The inclusion of particulars in *Wandering the Waste* helps to create the appearance of reality, only in the next scene to have that reality swept aside. Hayes's use of R.H. Stewart's art as a way of undermining his narrative is a perfect example of this,

"For instance the question of: did Raoul die of drinking contaminated water or from drinking cat's blood during an obscene ritual sacrifice. In the book we have Crowley explaining that Raoul died from drinking bad water in the captions while using the artwork to show the ceremony where the cat is sacrificed. I'm 99.9% sure that Raoul died from drinking contaminated water, but it's impossible to be 100% sure."

When I was approached to write a piece on a graphic novel about Aleister Crowley, "The Wickedest Man in the World", I think my heart gave a little jump. This is not Crowley's first appearance in the medium. Many graphic novels have had him in a supporting role or cameo, including Paul Jenkins's *Hellblazer*, and Alan Moore's *Promethea* and *From Hell*, but none that are dedicated to his life or putting him centre stage.

It is clear that Moore's work has been a huge influence on *Crowley*, and Hayes admits that, *"From Hell* had been in the back of my mind right from starting work on the outline."

There are many similarities between the two. Stewart's style is reminiscent of Eddie Campbell's, though at times suffers from a look or feel of being rushed. Also the use of annotations in *Crowley* (as in *From Hell*) is striking and elaborates on the text. It has been said that, given the graphic novel medium, such heavy use of annotations detracts from the primarily visual art form. Personally, I feel the form is quite capable of carrying the weight without them. Hayes, however, makes a justifiable case for their inclusion:

> "I can see why some people might have a problem with annotations in a graphic novel; certainly I wouldn't want to see them in every graphic novel I read. But in a well researched, historically accurate book I think they can only add to the whole. They're not being used to tell the story; only for background information which the reader may, hopefully, find interesting."

But even here one gets the impression that, as renowned Crowley biographer Richard Kaczynski notes in his foreword, despite being "untethered from the constraints of casting, location shots, and CGI budget" the medium struggles at times to do justice to the vastness of the subject matter. When asked about being limited by how much of Crowley he could portray in a single, 144-page volume, Hayes replied:

> "We try to cover the whole of AC's life in 100 pages. No easy task and the amount of juicy material that had to be left out is a little heartbreaking. You could easily fill 500 pages and barely scratch the surface. This was the main reason for doing chapter five 'Dreams Are

Nightmares and Waking Hours Delirium' as a fever dream; we're inside Crowley's thoughts as he lies desperately ill in bed. His mind reels and slips in time, we catch snatched glimpses of the myriad strange and fantastic things he has done which I didn't have space to fit into the book in a more fully realised way."

It is within this barrage in chapter five that we witness not only the high points of Crowley's multiple adventures, but also of Hayes's writing and Stewart's artwork. This chapter is skilfully written and illustrated, leaving one almost dizzy and in mind of Vonnegut's *Slaughterhouse-Five*.

As a graphic novel, or even a postmodern metafiction, it is extremely successful; however, for the fan boy in me who smiles at the myth Crowley created, it lacks insight into the man or his legend. But Hayes's approach is not without reason:

"I really didn't want to write a book that said either 'Here's all this bad stuff AC did, isn't he a bastard!' or 'Here's all this cool stuff AC did, isn't he ace!' Instead, I wanted to just present the known facts as best I could, along with the supernatural events which AC claimed to have witnessed, and let the reader make up their own mind as to what kind of man he may have been."

While this is a valid approach, the reader gains little more that a collage of snapshots from different works written about Crowley. One is aware of the vast amount of research that has gone into creating this work and can't help feeling that it would benefit from a greater degree of interpretation on the part of the author.

I asked Hayes about his own favourite story or myth surrounding Crowley, and now wish he had found a way to include it in the novel:

"I've always wished that Crowley's aborted attempt to design and construct a flying bicycle had come to fruition. The winged cycle would have been launched by pedalling it along a ramp that led through the woods on his Boleskine estate and down to the choppy waters of Loch Ness. The project was abandoned in the early design stages but I would have dearly loved to show the maiden flight in the book. It would have been majestic!"

My own favourite bit of Crowley, is the second half to his most quoted line. The first part is "Do what thou wilt shall be the whole of the Law", a line that continues to be used to illustrate the self-serving creed to do whatever you want. But the much less quoted second part to this refrain is "Love is the law, love under will"—a line which to this day I still find beautiful and with which Crowley signed off almost all of his correspondence—a line which, unfortunately, is missing from Hayes's work.

Whatever your option on Crowley the man or Crowley the myth, *Aleister Crowley: Wandering the Waste*, offers a superbly researched and well drawn introduction to the "The Wickedest Man in the World".

"Love is the law, love under will"

Matthew Stocker

଼

Not to be Taken at Bed-Time & Other Strange Stories
by Rosa Mulholland
Introduction by Richard Dalby
Sarob Press, May 2013, ix + 108 pages

On average, one hundred and forty-four respectable writers are forgotten annually, some sooner than others. In the case of Rosa Mulholland (later Lady Gilbert) the effect was almost instantaneous on her death in 1921. Her books fell quickly out of print despite their number, which included several reputable tomes, collections of poems, and bundles of short stories. However, despite this abundance, she was of that particularly vulnerable class: the Victorian Lady Novelist.

Born in Belfast, Mulholland grew up on High Street before moving to London to further herself. Here, she fell in with Charles Dickens, who encouraged her as a writer and visual artist, and requested her contribution to his periodical *All The Year Round*. The influence of, and association with, both Dickens and fellow contributor Wilkie Collins was formative; indeed, her novel *The Late Miss Hollingford* was serialised anonymously and wrongly attributed to both of her literary mentors until it was finally published years later under Mulholland's own name.

Like Dickens and Collins, Mulholland did not strictly include the supernatural as a mainstay of her fiction, although her sincere romanticism easily accommodates the gothic. Setting much of her prose in Ireland—although by no means all—allowed the unnatural and unholy in through the back door or, at least, in through the mouths of the peasants and backwater inhabitants of her homeland. In novels like the early *The Wild Woods of Toberevil* and the later *Banshee Castle*, this rustic superstition is drawn into focus, as it is in several of her short stories. During the publishing amnesia that came in the wake of her death, this is one area that still received at least a modicum of attention: of those Mulholland texts found easily online, the most prominent are her well-favoured spook tales; she appears twice in David Stuart Davies's *Best Irish Ghost Stories*.

In Sarob Press's *Not to be Taken at Bed-Time*, seven pieces of Mulholland's best supernatural fiction are compiled, some available elsewhere and others appearing in print for the first time in decades.

The collection succeeds in showing the diffuse and concentrated ways in which the supernatural permeates Mulholland's short writings. In certain contexts, it is the dressing of the story, in others the substantial meat. What remains her most-remembered story (and is here appropriately used as the collection's title) is "Not to be Taken at Bed-Time", a work that falls softly into the first category. The title, presumably a reference to Dickens's knowing ghostly tale "To be Taken With a Pinch of Salt", may be a sarcastic acknowledgement that the intention of the piece was not to scare or give the reader a bad night's sleep at all. It can be read, too, as a medical directive, commenting on the efficacy of the homespun remedies passed off, in the story, as possible cure-alls. Naturally they fail, as natural remedies often do.

In this tale, a Gaelic hermit finds himself unexpectedly in love with a young woman of Anglo-Irish stock. Unfortunately, he had already, long ago, foresworn to cause her father suffering and there's no undoing an oath made with fate, even when the heart wants otherwise. The hermit's efforts to court the girl pass from laboured good-doing to conspiracy with the local spaewoman, but all ends up the same: woman and wild man die, causing untold hurt to the grieving parent. When a duty is made with destiny, it cannot be unmade.

Whether the supernatural element here is the spaewoman's cause-and-effect or an over-seeing fate that ensures debts are paid is hard to say. If the author's intent was not to scare in the conventional sense, the prospect of a directing, forceful arm of destiny still unsettles in an unconventional way. Set amongst the beliefs of simple rustics, it conveys the same doomed fatalism as Thomas Hardy's "The Withered Arm", where fate is joined with station.

The uncanny feeling of the pre-ordained appears in other stories too, mostly in the form of reincarnation—old loves are reunited and ancient promises are kept by bodies within bodies within bodies. Elsewhere, apparitions ensure that fortunes are returned to their rightful inheritors. The tangibility of the supernature hardly matters: nothing will turn destiny from its intended course. In such a circumstance, belief in second lives, in ghosts, or in the local witch's *burragh-bos* are just speculative theories on how a super and natural force—fate, destiny, what have you—might actually be working.

There is meat here in pondering Mulholland's relationship with the Irish peasantry, whom she so regularly depicts. She is sympathetic, yes, and who amongst Dickens's coterie lacked a social conscious? However, the Presbyterian worldview of certainties unspoken in Mulholland's writing is not compatible with the pagan-catholic process of intercession that she frequently evokes. She views them with pity, the yokels, clearly understanding the folklore, if not the folk. They are a curiosity, but a curiosity she is close to; they are of the same time and place, but they see the world in different ways.

It is perhaps the force of this ideology—a belief in love, beauty, and that predetermination favours the fair—that lets Mulholland down the most: it allows no room for the truly horrific. It is a forceful ideology that is never written with force and, thus, the atmosphere that she creates initially always excites the imagination: a mysterious cliff top observatory in "The Mystery of Ora"; the appearance of a dead son's new Italian wife in "The Haunted Organist of Hurly Burly"; the fantasy of forgetful bliss that pervades the opening pages of "The Ghost at the Rath". Yet all the wild and beautiful flights of fancy are reined in and tied up nicely. The strange and the uncanny become the idealised.

If she is forgotten in her hometown, this may be why: Belfast is a place in which ideals clash and balance is never restored. It is a place that prefers writers to flag up faults and strengths, never to point out aims. It would never do, in Belfast, then, to admit that fate works out for the good, because there is a fear, unuttered in each of us here, that we and ours might be the bad guys. It does not do to speak of such things and a Novelist, a Victorian, a Lady should know better.

However, the point of this collection is not to frame Mulholland as a great Belfast writer or a great Irish writer, but to remember her as a writer of supernatural fiction. In this frame, she sits well. The prose is warm and generous, never likely to cause chills, but there is an estranging effect throughout. Everything is not quite right until it is set right. The restoration of the balance may not satisfy modern tastes, but the teetering of the scales, as if by some unseen hand, can be wonderfully affecting.

Special notice must be given of this first reprinting of "The Mystery of Ora", a memorable tale, previously forgotten. In it, Mulholland's greatest strengths are combined: an Irish setting and a cosiness that feels not quite right until fate intervenes. However, the weird, circular way in which fate plays out begs more questions of the force than it answers.

This collection of Rosa Mulholland's supernatural fiction is short and to the point. Seven pieces that, though divergent in their locations and their motivations, hint at a through-line that is still connected to Mulholland's wider body of work. It is discreet, sustained, and undemonstra-

tive, quietly paying tribute to a quiet talent. All which qualities seem wholly suitable here as they ever were in creatures,
like Mulholland, of that vulnerable class: the Victorian Lady
Novelist.

Reggie Chamberlain-King

જી

Vlad: A Novel
by Carlos Fuentes
Dalkey Archive Press, July 2012, 122 pages

Was Bram Stoker's *Dracula* a quintessentially "Irish" novel?
Some people think so, though the ravenous international
appetite for all things Draculesque would seem to argue
against such a limited cultural or geopolitical reading. No
Irish-language translation—that sure indicator of a special
nationalist significance—appeared until more than three decades after the novel's publication. Part of *Dracula*'s amazing
longevity has been its ability to reinvent itself over cultural
divides, whether though literary translation or theatrical/cin-
ematic adaptation.

Spanish iterations and imitations of Stoker's book have
been driven mostly by Hollywood films. The best-known
example is Universal's simultaneously produced Spanish-
language version of the 1931 Tod Browning classic starring
Bela Lugosi. Although in many ways technically superior,
the clashing accents of performers from Spain, Mexico, and
Argentina at the dawn of talkies raised all sorts of questions
about national origin and authenticity.

Carlos Fuentes's final published book of fiction, *Vlad* is
billed as "A Novel", although novella or even novelette would
be a better description. It also presents itself as doing some-

thing insightfully Mexican with Stoker's template, but it borrows so heavily from an overused playbook of vampire tropes and clichés that the geographical location becomes almost irrelevant. We enter a very familiar Dracula-land—meaning here no real place in particular.

A version of *Vlad* first appeared in English in 2004, in *Playboy*, though the present translation, by E. Shaskan Bumas and Alejandro Branger, is copyrighted 2012. At 122 pages, almost exactly the length of a screenplay, Fuentes's ficcione reads as if it would much rather exist as a film, and it would be mostly a matter of reformatting dialogue to produce a filmable script. But that doesn't mean it would make a good movie. The plot centres on Yves Navarro, senior partner in a Mexico City law firm headed by the aging Don Eloy Zurinaga, who conducts his business affairs mostly in absentia. He assigns Navarro the task of finding a suitable home for an old-world friend, Count Vlad Radu, who has been stripped of his land holdings and driven into exile by Eastern European conflict. Navarro's wife Asunción is a real estate broker, and she finds a secluded house for Count Vlad which he renders windowless, and installs industrial style drains in the floor.

By this time only the densest (or most culturally deprived) reader cannot know exactly who Vlad is and what he might be up to. Finished with Stoker's drained template, Fuentes turns to Francis Ford Coppola, whose *Bram Stoker's Dracula* (1992) provides both Vlad the Impaler and reincarnation backstories, although the parallel life business involves children this time. It is doubtful, however, that even by the permissive standards of today's major media conglomerates, we could ever see an onscreen representation of two girls, one ten years old and one ten-going-on-five hundred, exploring the playtime possibilities of stuffing hungry rats into their panties.

Along the way, Fuentes does manage to conjure some occasionally striking images—such as the surprising revelation (spoiler alert) that Vlad has no eyes behind his sun shades, just empty sockets, and perceives the world extrasensorily. Scenes like this would delight the makeup effects people. But they would have difficulty with other details. The author (or his translators) never decides whether the vampire's fingernails are translucent or transparent, and the reader can't either. Fuentes occasionally descends into the realm of cutesy-pieness, as when, adding to the list of familiar Slavic and quasi-Slavic supernatural nomenclature like "the nosferatu", "the strigoi", and "the muroni", he introduces a groaning lower-case invention, "the lugosi". Other in-the-know references include "one of the last remaining Porfirian mansions", apparently inspired by the disease Porphyria, a condition regularly seized upon by tabloid television to explain the belief in vampires, but almost universally dismissed by folklorists.

The dust flap copy for *Vlad* describes the book as a figurative examination of middle-class Mexican malaise in an increasingly lawless country. The problem is, beyond a few lines in which Vlad delights in a "city without police protection! You wouldn't believe the trouble Scotland Yard put me through . . . " the novel never develops these themes at all. Carlos Fuentes was a great modern figure in Mexican literature, a leading stylist and justifiably acclaimed practitioner of magical realism. He doesn't deserve to be remembered by this book. One wishes he had more fully developed the fascinating character of Don Eloy Zurinaga. At the engaging outset, the reader will likely assume (hope) that the eccentric old lawyer himself is Vlad, but instead we are forced to settle for a tired, standard-issue Dracula of which we didn't really need another copy.

David J. Skal

Ghost of Shandon
Story and art by Alan Corbett
On Stream Publications Ltd, 2012, 64 pages

Ronan is a lonely, unhappy child; a newcomer to present-day Cork, bullied and made fun of at school where he is considered a country bumpkin. He escapes through reading, his favourite book being *The Three Musketeers*. One day, he is sitting with his book in a former graveyard, now a park, when a strange figure appears: "with pale white skin and faded clothing . . . there was a ghostly air about her". It is Aisling, a girl from the eighteenth-century when Cork was a cosmopolitan port, with influential Dutch, French Huguenot and British residents as well as the indigenous Irish. When Ronan leaves the graveyard with Aisling, he realises that something very peculiar has happened: the streets have changed and are filled with oddly-clad people. Somehow Ronan has slipped back in time to 1792, and Aisling, who believes he is a faerie, takes him to the local apothecary for advice. Eventually Ronan manages to convince them both that he is from the future, but there is bad news: in order to get back home, he must first acquire "a drop of an ancient potion made from the water of the Dead Sea. This must fall on the keys to the city which must be then turned in the city's oldest doors, where Cork began in the seventh-century, at St. Finn Barre's Cathedral". The rest of the story revolves around Ronan and Aisling's hunt to obtain the keys; an adventure complicated by the fact that "more sinister faeries might have followed" Ronan through time. Specifically this is the horrible Dualachan, "a dark faerie that raced through the land . . . It had no face or eyes to call its own so it would search desperately, hunting for the eyes of lost souls". We also learn more about Aisling and her love of old stories; her fantasies of fighting pirates like the famous Ann Bonny. And there is the secretive and powerful Friendly Club, membership of which is much sought-after by the businessmen in the city.

Above all, however, the reader discovers—in a fairly painless, non-didactic way—a good deal about old Cork and its history, for this graphic novel has an intended audience of children aged eight and over. The artist/author, Alan Corbett, has an MA in children's book illustration and has worked as a teacher. *Ghost of Shandon* is provided with an annotated map, and the locations in the novel are identified in headings, so that anyone can follow the events *in situ*. I have visions of school classes wandering the streets of Cork, discovering the (doubtless innumerable) differences between the city as it was in the eighteenth-century and as it is now. This can only be a good thing. When I read the publicity for the book, I was concerned about the statement that Alan Corbett had written it "in language easily understood by the children of ages he has taught in schools over the years". Talking or writing down to young people is a recipe for disaster, but in practice this is not a major problem here: how could it be in a story that involves an *apothecary* (hardly a word that an average modern eight-year-old encounters every day)?

The artwork in *Ghost of Shandon* is interesting, although it seems to owe little to one of Alan Corbett's stated inspirations: the great Harry Clarke. The technique is a sort of pastel wash, and for my taste the figures of the two central characters are too cutesy, but the set-pieces and the detailed portrayals of locations are atmospheric. The full-page apothecary's shop is nicely bedecked with skulls and bottles, the mask stall in the market is inviting, and the street scenes make one want to join Ronan and Aisling in their adventures. Nor are punches pulled with the depiction of the Dualachan, who is dark and quite nasty as he careers around the streets in his bone-decorated black carriage. [See the front cover illustration of this issue. –ed.] But is he what he appears to be? I'm afraid not, for herein lies the disappointment of the book as far as I'm concerned. Perhaps the author feels that young children should not be offered the possibility that horrible creatures from (real or imaginary) folklore might just exist. Instead we're given a cop-out Scooby-Doo type resolution. Certainly the plot holds together in its simple way, but even in a book for youngish children I might have hoped for a little more sophistication, a little more risk-taking. At the end Ronan steps "into a new world" and we are told that his adventures are "to be continued". So maybe next time Alan Corbett will be a bit bolder.

Rosemary Pardoe

৪৩

Everything is Always Wrong
by Graham Tugwell
Self-published, April 2013, 67 pages

Tugwell's self-described "collectionette", *Everything is Always Wrong*, gathers five disparate stories from his extensive body of work. What results is a somewhat mixed bag of fiction; unfortunately unremarkable in parts, but engaging, intriguing, and disturbing when at its best.

Before launching into the stories themselves, a brief prologue asks us to internalise three rules that govern Tugwell's world: 1) There is No God, 2) Love is Impossible, 3) The Universe is Malign.

"Now, off you go", it finishes, neatly combining Tugwell's two main modes of storytelling: a concern with depicting a vicious and unsentimental reality, and a clear delight in threading it through with a sense of humour. The collection reaches its high point when he manages to strike a balance between darkness and comedy, but many of the stories veer too far in one direction or the other, resulting in an uneven tone and lack of coherence which prevents it from leaving any serious overall impression on the reader.

The opening story, for example, skews excessively towards the absurd, relying heavily on a central conceit that doesn't quite manage to hold the narrative aloft. In short, "Romancing the Crab" charts the rather awkward progression of a new relationship, with one obvious difference—one half of the couple is a crab. Although Tugwell does manage to exploit the absurdity of the situation for laughs, the initial uncanniness quickly fades, and the reader is left to plough through twenty very straightforward pages of awkward romance for little gratification.

In contrast, a piece that comes later in the collection, "High Five, Danny O'C", manages to ramp up the humour in a more engaging manner, showcasing Tugwell's own brand of bizarre speculative fiction to much greater effect. Casting nineteenth-century Irish political leader, Daniel O'Connell, as the time-travelling Liberator (or perhaps a figment of the imagination) of a young Irish boy longing to escape the stifling atmosphere of his small-town home, it riffs nicely on themes of rebellion and acting-out, and toys with metafiction in the form of Wikipedia-style [citation needed] inserts. Although it depends on obvious absurdity for humour just as much as "Romancing the Crab"—Daniel O'Connell conspiring with the boy to "write a couple of rude words on Jesus' chest", for example—it's a more substantial read than the previous story, and doesn't lose steam in the same way once the initial sense of absurdity wears off.

Perhaps the biggest misstep of the collection, however, is the inclusion of "Unskin Me with Your Neck of Knives". Lacking the humour of both "Romancing the Crab" and "High Five, Danny O'C", as well as the bleakly realistic edge that makes the latter an interesting read, it opts instead for a mix of surrealism and eroticism, which—although suited to the piece as an isolated story—jars with Tugwell's other selections. And in such a short collection, even a small incongruity throws off the book's overall tone and cohesion significantly.

While *Everything is Always Wrong* may have its weak points, the two remaining stories are compelling enough to ensure that it feels like a worthwhile read. "They've Come to Paint the Doors Again", the book's closing story, is a more straightforward horror piece than any of the others, but it does what it does brilliantly. Relying on evocation rather than explicit detail to build tension, it charts the effects of an unspecified, likely supernatural infection on the lives of a man and his daughter. It's the kind of story comprised mostly of gaps, in which the experience of what is left unsaid is far more horrifying than the actual events described, and it leaves a lasting impression along with a genuine sense of unease.

Even better than "They've Come to Paint the Doors Again", though, is "We Left Him with the Dragging Man". Arguably the high point of the collection, this story is distinctly reminiscent of Jerome Bixby's "It's a Good Life", and is an excellent demonstration of Tugwell's aptitude for blending horror with the mundane. It charts the friendship of five boys who come together "because no-one else would have us", and the increasingly destructive actions of one member of their group, Alby Gorman. Gorman is Tugwell's stand-in for Anthony Freemont; comprised of a sinister jumble of childhood whims and terrifying supernatural abilities, he takes a worrying pleasure from exerting control over his peers in increasingly harmful ways. As tensions escalate, his four companions decide that something needs to be done: "We can leave him with the Dragging Man." The Dragging Man, it turns out, is a nightmarish creature living in a derelict house in the nearby woods, luring unsuspecting visitors into the darkness to face a murky end. Tricking Gorman into a camping trip, the boys leave him in the monster's clutches. But when they return out of guilt soon after, they find the Dragging Man in his death-throes. "He got out," it explains. It's here, in playing with a mixture of the sinister and the grimly absurd, that Tugwell really finds a balance that does his writing justice.

Although *Everything is Always Wrong* never quite comes together as a unified collection, its stronger moments do justify the small time-investment required to read this slim volume in its entirety. Tugwell clearly has immense breadth as a writer of speculative fiction, and this first collection of his stories—despite its flaws—is worth picking up as an introduction to his extensive body of work, and for a quick, concentrated dose of horror and humour.

Emily Bourke

∞

Harry Clarke: The Life and Work
by Nicola Gordon Bowe
The History Press Ireland, 2012; 384 pages

This splendid book first saw the light of day as the author's PhD thesis for Trinity College, Dublin in 1984. It was promptly submitted under the aegis of the Irish Antique Dealers' Association to the Confédération Internationale des Négociants en Oeuvres d'Art in Brussels and won that organisation's 1984 Prize "in recognition of an academic publication or a remarkable contribution to furthering the cultural preservation through art works in a CINOA member country" five years before its first edition appeared from Irish Academic Press during Clarke's centenary in 1989. Two further editions of the book appeared in 1994 and 2004.

A well-thumbed copy of the first edition sits on my shelf, and if that edition was a revelation, this revised and updated edition is the very model of what I always wish for but seldom find in a book devoted to an artist I admire. The large format trade paperback is securely bound and printed on glossy paper that does not smear when you touch the page. The first edition had reprinted a large selection of Clarke's work in all the modes in which he worked from stained glass to paintings to graphic art, and in all the venues in which it appeared from ecclesiastical installations to civic institutions, private commissions, posters, advertisements, magazines, and the lavishly illustrated books for which he is best known outside Ireland. Drafts offering insight into Clarke's methods of composition were included alongside completed works. Equally interesting was the selection of works by artists who influenced Clarke or to whom he paid homage. Bowe made striking use of comparisons to demonstrate how the artist assimilated motifs and gestures in various art forms as varied in age, style, and expression as the anonymous sculptors and glass-workers responsible for the microcosmic world decorating nearly every nook and cranny of medieval cathedrals, the stylised decadence and ornamental surfaces of Aubrey Beardsley's drawings and the Symbolist Gustav Klimt's paintings, as well as the grotesquerie of Friedrich Wilhelm Murnau's Expressionist film *Nosferatu.* As welcome as these illustrations were in earlier editions of this book, a majority of them had been rather small and in black and white, with two sets of colour plates.

The present edition reproduces many more illustrations than had appeared previously, presents them in their original colour scheme and in larger formats, adds details from particularly complex or large illustrations, and places them all adjacent to the text describing them. Reproduction had been good in earlier editions, though limited by the paper-stock on which most of them had been placed and their size. All of the reproductions in this new edition are superb, the colours rich, details sharp, the blacks an abyss from which anything could emerge. Clarke's illustrations for Goethe's *Faust* have been favourites of mine since I first encountered them in the late 1970s; however, the colour illustration "The Witch's Kitchen" had usually been reproduced as a brown blur with a blue-clad Faust, a red-clad Mephistopheles, and the Witch's pale grey flesh emerging from a mostly indeterminate background. As shown here, the kitchen is home to a welter of contorted organic matter, dripping from the ceiling, staring from the corners, bulbous and rotten, attempting to coalesce into some abominable incarnation. Just as remarkable is the level of detail captured in the famous image of Poe's M. Valdemar awakening from his trance, where every pore seems to exude putrescence, writhing fetuses decorate the dress of the saturnine woman standing beside the bed, and the darkness pressing in on the figures around the bedside is relieved only by a single figure silhouetted against an open doorway in the upper right corner, an ominous counterpart to the benign figure striking a similar pose in Diego Velázquez's "*Las Meninas*".

Nonetheless, everything here is not dark, distorted or damned, though Clarke is wont to occasionally add grotesques to even the most glorious of his ecclesiastical stained glass fixtures, just as he includes illustrations depicting moments of transcendence and beauty in his otherwise very dark work for Poe and Goethe. One excellent example is the vignette that follows the "Easter Hymn" in *Faust*, which depicts a symbolic landscape with a simple but beautiful illustration of Christ's ascension attended by angels and arms reaching down from heaven on the right and a dark hill disclosing the glowering eyes of hell on the left. Bowe calls attention to Clarke's "dualistic medieval fascination with mystical heavenly beauty contrasted with worm-ridden rotten evil". This seeming dissonance works in Clarke's art, as it does with the artisans in the medieval cathedrals, and later artists like Bosch and Brueghel, because he creates, as Bowe states, "dreamed images imbued with iconic substance", a world where the rational and irrational, the realistic and fantastic, the grotesque, the arabesque, and the numinous meet and freely interact with each other. Here intricate and prodigious detail contrasts with expanses of pure white or black, the ignoble Judas finds succor at the hands of the noble St. Brendan, the chaste Marguerite falls prey to but eventually redeems the decadent Faust, intolerance and superstition yields to love and freedom on the Eve of St. Agnes, and the rich panoply of Irish literature from poetry to prose to drama can leap into gorgeous life through the panels of the Geneva Window.

Bowe covers Clarke's life and the world which shaped it in meticulous, but consistently interesting detail from his apprenticeship in glass-making following the nadir of stained glass in the late nineteenth-century; through the destruction of his first book (an illustrated edition of Samuel Taylor Coleridge's "Rime of the Ancient Mariner") during the 1916 Easter Rising; through the ensuing years of success in stained glass and illustration, overwork, illness, frustration over the evasive reception of his Geneva Window and death due to tuberculosis at the age of forty-one, one year younger than his mother had been when she died of the same disease when the artist was fourteen years old. The book concludes with a 1928 article, "Some Notes on Stained Glass" "based on information supplied by Harry Clarke", a "List of Stained Glass Windows by Harry Clarke", copious notes, and a helpful index. Even if you already have an earlier edition of this book, I cannot recommend it highly enough.

Jim Rockhill

Notes on Contributors

Emily Bourke is a recent graduate of the MPhil in Popular Literature at Trinity College Dublin, where she wrote her dissertation on the Gothic in contemporary fantasy literature. She currently works in communications, but hopes to pursue a PhD in the not-too-distant future.

Nicola Gordon Bowe, former Lecturer in Design History and founding Director of the MA in History of Design and the Applied Arts at the National College of Art & Design in Dublin, is now Associate Fellow at NCAD, and Associate Professor at the University of Ulster. An Honorary Fellow of the British Society of Master Glass Painters, she has published and lectured widely, especially on the Arts and Crafts revivals in early twentieth-century Ireland within an international context.

Reggie Chamberlain-King is a Belfast-based writer, broadcaster, musiphilosoph, and humble savant. His first novel, *A Poisoned Chalice for Charlie*, was received warmly by the back of a drawer. He has worked previously with the staff of the BBC, Ulster Bank, and Royal Mail and may do so again. He also makes regular appearances on public transport.

Scott Connors is an independent scholar who has twice been nominated for the International Horror Guild Award for editing books by and about Clark Ashton Smith. He has also written for *Lovecraft Annual*, *Studies in Weird Fiction*, *Weird Fiction Review*, *All Hallows*, *Ghost and Scholars*, *The Explicator*, and *Publishers Weekly*. He has contributed to such books as *Supernatural Literature of the World*, *Warnings to the Curious*, *Icons of Supernatural Horror*, *The Robert E. Howard Reader*, *The Barbaric Triumph*, and *Encyclopedia of the Vampire*. He lives in northern California.

Richard Dalby is a widely-respected editor, anthologist, and scholar of supernatural fiction. He has edited collections by E.F. Benson, H.R. Wakefield, Bram Stoker, and Rosa Mulholland; and his numerous anthologies include *Dracula's Brood*, *Victorian Ghost Stories by Eminent Women Writers*, and *Victorian and Edwardian Ghost Stories*.

Steve Gronert Ellerhoff is an Iowan. His short fiction has appeared in *Fourteen Hills*, *The Adroit Journal*, and *P. Q. Leer*. A graduate of the creative writing MA at Lancaster University, he also holds an MPhil in Literatures of the Americas from Trinity College Dublin, where he is now finishing a PhD exploring myth in the short fiction of Ray Bradbury and Kurt Vonnegut. His novel, *Time's Laughingstocks*, launched in September.

Rosemary Pardoe began the small press journal *Ghosts & Scholars* (or *The Ghosts & Scholars M.R. James Newsletter* in its current incarnation) in 1979. She has edited and written several books, the most recent of which is *The Ghosts & Scholars Book of Shadows*, containing new sequels and prequels to James's stories by various authors. A second volume is planned for 2014. She *does* have other interests!

Albert Power is a gothic scholar and author. He has written articles for *Wormwood* and edited fiction by Sheridan Le Fanu and Thomas Leland for Swan River Press. He has regularly given public presentations on gothic writers. His own shorter fiction has been published by Ex Occidente Press. His novel *Slaver Heap* and collection *Daring Savishna* are forthcoming in 2014.

Jim Rockhill has edited volumes collecting the supernatural fiction of Joseph Sheridan Le Fanu, Bob Leman, and E.T.A. Hoffmann; co-edited Jane Rice's weird tales, and *Reflections in a Glass Darkly*. He has also contributed to books by Seabury Quinn and Brian J. Showers; as well as *Supernatural Literature of the World*, *The Freedom of Fantastic Things*, *Warnings to the Curious*, *Encyclopedia of the Vampire*, *All Hallows*, *Dead Reckonings*, and *Le Fanu Studies*.

Brian J. Showers has written short stories, articles, interviews, and reviews for magazines such as *Rue Morgue*, *Supernatural Tales* and *Wormwood*. His collection *The Bleeding Horse* won the Children of the Night Award in 2008. He is also the author of *Literary Walking Tours of Gothic Dublin*; and, with Gary W. Crawford and Jim Rockhill, he co-edited the Stoker Award-nominated *Reflections in a Glass Darkly: Essays on J. Sheridan Le Fanu*.

David J. Skal is an author, lecturer, and documentary film-maker whose many books include *Hollywood Gothic*, *The Monster Show*, *V is for Vampire*, and *Screams of Reason*. He is co-author (with Elias Savada) of *Dark Carnival: The Secret World of Tod Browning*, and, with Nina Auerbach, co-editor of the Norton Critical Edition of Bram Stoker's *Dracula*. He has lectured widely and taught courses based on his books at the University of Victoria and Trinity College Dublin. His current project is a cultural biography, *Bram Stoker: The Final Curtain*, to be published in 2014.

Matthew Stocker is the pseudonym of a graduate of Trinity College's School of English. He was an avid researcher of the occult for many years. His wife made him stop. Matthew worked in the book trade for over ten years, until he sold one eReader too many. He wishes to remain anonymous because he now works in web development. Matthew lives under the kitchen table and tells stories for food.

Book Stalls

Welcome to the Book Stalls. Here are a few titles of interest from our favourite booksellers. Feel free to browse and contact sellers for further information and shipping rates. When ordering, please mention *The Green Book*.

Richard Dalby
4 Westbourne Park, Scarborough
North Yorkshire YO12 4AT, UK
+44 (0)1723 377049

Brennan, Elizabeth. *Whispering Walls*. Dublin: Metropolitan Press, 1948. 1st ed.; very good. Gothic Irish novel. £15

Hone, Joseph, ed. *Irish Ghost Stories*. Hamish Hamilton, 1977. 1st ed.; ex-library, good reading copy in d/j. Ten stories by Brian Moore, John McGahern, William Trevor, etc. £6

Le Fanu, J.S. *Spalatro—Two Italian Tales*. Sarob Press, 2001. limited to 250 copies, fine in fine d/j. Includes "Spalatro" and "Borrhomeo the Astrologer", edited and introduced by Miles Stribling. £25

O'Donnell, Elliott. *Haunted Waters*. Rider, 1957. 1st ed.; very good in very good d/j. Inscription on endpaper. £20

Stoker, Bram. *Midnight Tales*. Peter Owen, 1990. 1st ed.; fine in fine d/j. £12

The Swan River Press
swanriverpress.ie / brian@swanriverpress.ie
All prices inclusive of international postage.

Leland, Thomas. *Longsword, Earl of Salisbury* [1762]. Edited by Albert Power. Dublin: Swan River Press, 2012. Signed by editor. Jacketed hardback. New. €30

Le Fanu, J. S. *The Ballads and Poems of J. Sheridan Le Fanu.* Dublin: Swan River Press, 2011. 1st ed., hand-sewn pamphlet. New. €13

Le Fanu, J. S. *The Complete Ghost Stories of Chapelizod.* Edited by Albert Power. Dublin: Swan River Press, 2011. 1st ed., hand-sewn pamphlet. New. €13

[Le Fanu, J. S.] *Joseph Sheridan Le Fanu—A Concise Bibliography.* By Gary W. Crawford and Brian J. Showers. Dublin: Swan River Press, 2011. 1st ed., staple-bound pamphlet. New. €10

Le Fanu, J. S. *My Aunt Margaret's Adventure.* Introduction and annotations by Jim Rockhill; afterword by Gary W. Crawford. Dublin: Swan River Press, 2009. 1st ed., hand-sewn pamphlet. New. €10

Showers, Brian J. *The Bleeding Horse and Other Ghost Stories.* Cork: Mercier Press, 2008. Signed by author. 1st ed., jacketed hardback. New. €20

Showers, Brian J. *Old Albert—An Epilogue* [2011]. Dublin: Swan River Press, 2012. Signed by author. 1st ed., jacketed hardback. New. €25

Showers, Brian J. *Literary Walking Tours of Gothic Dublin*. Dublin: Nonsuch, 2006. Signed by author, 1st ed., paperback. New €22.

[Stoker, Bram.] *Bram Stoker's Other Gothics—Contemporary Reviews*. Introduction by Carol A. Senf. Dublin: Swan River Press, 2010. 1st ed., hand-sewn pamphlet. New. €10

[Stoker, Bram.] *Contemporary Reviews of "Dracula"*. Introduction by Leah Moore and John Reppion. Dublin: Swan River Press, 2011. 1st ed., hand-sewn pamphlet. New. €10

Stoker, Bram. *The Definitive Judge's House*. Frontispiece and introduction by Mike Mignola. Endnotes and afterword by Jack G. Voller. Dublin: Swan River Press, 2011. 1st ed., hand-sewn pamphlet. New. €10

Stoker, Bram. *Extracts from Personal Reminiscences of Henry Irving by Bram Stoker*. Selected and introduced by Elizabeth Miller. Dublin: Swan River Press, 2010. 1st ed., hand-sewn pamphlet. New. €10

Stoker, Bram. *Four Romances by Mr. Bram Stoker*. Introduction by Paul Murray. Dublin: Swan River Press, 2010. 1st ed., hand-sewn pamphlet. New. €10

[Stoker, Bram.] *Thirty Years A-Going: A History of the Bram Stoker Society*. By Albert Power. Dublin: Swan River Press, 2009. 1st ed., staple-bound pamphlet. New. €10

Stoker, Bram and Hall Caine. *To My Dear Friend Hommy-Beg: The Great Friendship of Bram Stoker and Hall Caine*. Introduction by Richard Dalby. Dublin: Swan River Press, 2011. 1st ed., hand-sewn pamphlet. New. €10